Yang Hu
Xiao Yang

Cultural China Series

CHINESE PUBLISHING

Homeland of Printing

Translated by Zha Xiaoyun & Lei Jing

CHINA
INTERCONTINENTAL
PRESS

图书在版编目（CIP）数据

中国书业；英文／杨虎，肖阳著；查晓云，雷静译.—北京：五洲传播出版社，2010.1

ISBN 978-7-5085-1315-7

I.中... II.①杨...②肖...③查...④雷... III.出版工作－文化史－中国－英文 IV.G239.29

中国版本图书馆CIP数据核字（2008）第058087号

CHINESE PUBLISHING
Homeland of Printing

Author: Yang Hu & Xiao Yang
Translator: Zha Xiaoyun & Lei Jing
Pictures Editor: Zhou Jing
Executive Editor: Gao Lei
Art Director: Tian Lin
Publisher: China Intercontinental Press (6 Beixiaomachang, Lianhuachi Donglu, Haidian District, Beijing 100038, China)
Tel: 86-10-58891281
Website: www.cicc.org.cn
Printer: C&C Joint Printing Co., (Beijing) Ltd.
Format: 720×965mm 1/16
Edition: Jan. 2010, 1st edition, 1st print run
Price: RMB 99.00 (*yuan*)

目　录

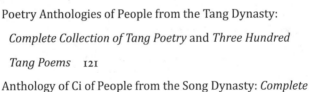

Preface: Three-thousand-year History of Books in China

Publishing activities are significant to human civilization. Different civilizations breed distinct publishing activities, whereas publishing activities advance civilizations.

The time-honored Chinese civilization has nurtured the distinctive Chinese publishing industry. To some extent, its formulation and development mimics that of Chinese civilization. Featured with long historical standing, plenty of connotations, unity of styles, extensive influences and constant innovation, Chinese civilization is unique in the world in its continuity.

Ancient China not only produced brilliant achievements for human civilization, but also has been showed a tendency towards strong development and flourishing prospects through almost a hundred years of reform and development. As the old Chinese saying notes: "Although Zhou was an ancient state, it had undertaken a mission to reform."

This tendency has partly determined the unique characteristics of the development of China's publishing industry's. At the same time, publishing, as a significant activity of knowledge accumulation and cultural inheritance, has contributed greatly to the spread and inheritance of Chinese civilization. From a broader view, as one of the earliest countries with the most advanced publishing industry, ancient China played an important role in the history of world publishing. In the past thousands of years, Chinese civilization has spread all over the world with books as carriers and has taken a significant part in the development of world culture by constructing the Asian Confucianism civilization circle. Especially, the invention and spread of papermaking and printing techniques have contributed to human civilization and have profoundly influenced the development of human society.

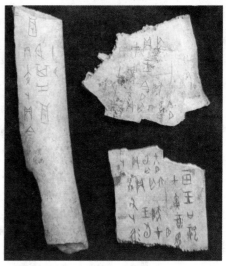

Oracle bone pieces with inscriptions

The written language, a foremost recording tool of knowledge and culture, is the prerequisite for a publishing industry. China is a country that has had many different nationalities and languages since ancient times. Among the numerous character systems, Chinese characters are the mainstay for the spread and inheritance of Chinese civilization. Among all the written languages of the Four Great Ancient Civilizations, the Chinese written language had a stable character outline, explicit meaning and good continuity. Because of Chinese written language, today's people can both understand different kinds of books written in the past thousands

Bronze movable-type print from the Ming Dynasty (1368–1644) —Cao Zijian's Collection years and depict fluently today's changing and fast developing world. Thanks to Chinese characters, Chinese civilization has been extended for thousands of years without any interruption.

After the appearance of the written language as a carrier of knowledge, the pressing problem plaguing the development of the publishing industry was to find the appropriate recording material for the written language. After trying bamboo, wood, oracle bone, bronze, stone and silk, Chinese people invented paper to write and paint around the 2nd century B.C. This was an epoch-making invention because paper is the best writing material that has been ever found on earth.

In 105 A.D., the gradual spread of papermaking technique, innovated by Cai Lun, enormously promoted the development of the publishing industry and society. Inspired by the rubbing and sealing techniques, Chinese people invented printing technique in the 7th century B.C. That led to new progress on the quality and quantity of book publishing and brought the history of human communication and civilization to a new stage. During 1041–1049 A.D., the civilian Bi Sheng invented typography, the printing-type material which transferred from plaster to wood to metal such as copper, tin and others. In the 11st century, registration printing came into being on the basis of engraving, which made printed matter more attractive and plentiful.

Well connected with the constant innovation of the character carrier and replica technique, the Chinese publishing industry enjoyed continuous development. From the 21st century B.C. to 16th century B.C., Chinese publishing was burgeoning and it experienced a historical transformation from the written language to primary publication. Then primary editions and classical collections appeared, as well as the appearance of some initial elements of publication. It is conservatively estimated that the Chinese publishing industry has a history of over 3000 years.

The early compilation activities followed, in which Chinese

Jianyang copy of *Zhou Bi Suan Jing*, during the Song Dynasty (960–1279).

Brand mark of *The Kai Feng Story* during the Song Dynasty

people accumulated rich compiling experience and developed their own compiling methods. The invention of papermaking technique, that later become a major category in ancient Chinese handicrafts, fundamentally changed the media of the written language.

Five major publishing systems were gradually established after the appearance of printing technique. They were official publications from government publishing houses; bookshop publications from private publishing houses; personal publications; academy publications from academy publishing houses and temple and monastery publications. The boom of the publishing industry promoted book circulation and trade. In the 2nd century B.C., Shu Si (书肆)—the early book marketplace, came to existence in Chang'an and other economically and culturally developed cities. Book businesses gradually flourished during

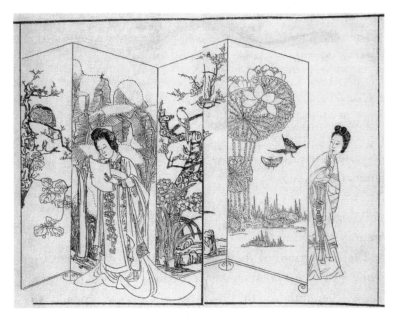

An illustration of A Secret Copy of *Bei Xi Xiang* published in the 13th year of Emperor Chong Zhen in the Ming Dynasty (1639)

the Tang and Song dynasties (618–1279) and various business methods including advertising were used. During the Southern Song Dynasty (127–1279), the idea and practice of copyright entered the Chinese book industry. The earliest copyright mark was in the brand mark of the book *The Kai Feng Story* (《东都事略》) (published in 1190–1194), on which 15 characters were written, reading "first published by Cheng from Mt. MeiShan, registered already, no unauthorized copy is allowed."

The significant achievement of ancient Chinese publishing is that publications are large in number and rich in connotation, with various forms and far-reaching influence. Hence, it has become one of the remarkable symbols of Chinese civilization.

China has a fine tradition of "valuing knowledge and honoring writing." Since ancient times, Chinese intellectuals have devoted themselves to writing to express faith, attain pride and earn fame. Statistics show that there are some 2.3 million volumes of 180,000 kinds from the Western Han Dynasty to the Qing Dynasty (202 B.C.–1911 A.D.). Ancient Chinese books have various categories. Under Confucian classics, history, philosophy, literature, Buddhism

Books of different layouts published by the governmental organizations in the Qing Dynasty

and Taoism scriptures, there are diverse types of literature. Giant works with many volumes symbolize the grandness of ancient Chinese literature and the prosperity of the publishing industry. For instance, great works like the *Yongle Encyclopedia* of the Ming Dynasty (1368–1644 with 370 million words), *The Compendium of Works of Past and Present* of the Qing Dynasty (1616–1911), the *Imperial Collection of Four* (nearly 1 billion words) were the classics. Chinese books, particular about beauty in form, have bamboo and wooden slips, scrolls and album book systems with various bookbinding forms consisting of folding forms, whirlwind binding, dragon-scale binding, butterfly-like binding, wrapped-ridge binding and traditional thread binding. In addition, Chinese books have elegant regard for paper and ink, style, and format.

Cherishing books and old scriptures is one of fine traditions in Chinese culture. But owing to both human and natural factors, all the ancient Chinese books have experienced a tough time, and suffered heavy losses in the historic process, which have stirred even greater efforts in collecting and protecting books.

As an important part of Chinese publishing, collections in China started early and developed deeply. Collecting systems evolved among feudal officials, private persons, Buddhist and

Taoist temples and academies of classical learning. In ancient China, there were millions of private libraries and bibliophiles contributed brilliantly to book maintenance, repairing and protection. As a result, a distinct book-keeping culture has developed.

Ancient Chinese have accumulated rich experience in writing, publishing, maintaining and reading books. Through research on books, "a study of publishing" has formed which is focusing on making printing blocks; distinguishing authentic writings from imitations; collecting; emendating; table of contents; and so on. The numerous researches on these fields have increased the academic value of ancient publishing.

China, historically, has stressed communication with other countries. Publication exchanges are an important means of communication. "The Book Road" was been built across Asia and Europe during long periods of cross-country communication.

Library of Yue Lu Academy in Hunan Province: the Yu Shu Building

As a result, China spread its advanced publishing technique together with its science and culture, and also learned a lot from other countries and areas, which has promoted the progress of Chinese civilization. China and the rest of the world influenced each other and achieved harmonious development.

Although ancient Chinese publishing took the leading position in the world for a long time and exerted widespread influence especially in the publishing industries of countries in the Confucianism Civilization circle, the influence of Chinese publishing decreased in modern times, even below the advanced world level for a while.

From the 19th century onwards, with western learning spreading to the east, the Chinese publishing industry realized a successful transition through learning from and drawing lessons from western-developed publishing.

Founded in 1897 and 1912 respectively, the Commercial Press and Zhonghua Book Company have become the new publishing companies keeping abreast of the times by actively improving technology and adopting the operation and management style of capitalism. In the first half of 20th century, the Chinese publishing industry achieved a revolution from traditional to modernized and merged into the development trend of world publishing industry with brand-new outlook. From then on, modern publishing has become the main form of Chinese publishing and it has entered into a splendid development period.

After the founding of People's Republic of China in 1949, modern publishing has achieved greater accomplishments. With 60 years of development, China has become a power in the global publishing industry.

First, the scale of the publishing industry is

Book Disaster
Book disaster means man-made damages to official collecting books in ancient China. As early as in Sui Dynasty, Niu Hong had the view of "Five Disasters": the first was "Burning books" by Qin Shihuang in the Qin Dynasty; the second "Chimei" rebellion army entering the Central Plains at the end of West Han Dynasty; the third "Dongzhuo shifting capital" in Three Kingdoms Period, the fourth Liu (Liu Yuan) and Shi(Shi Le)'s Rebellion in Northern and Southern Dynasties; the fifth "Burning books" in Jiangling by Emperor Yuan of Liang in the Sothern Dynasty. Later, in the Ming Dynasty, Hu Yinglin added another five on to it, and they were: the sixth was "Burning books" in Jiangdu at the end of the Sui Dynasty; the seventh "the An Lushan Rebellion"in Tang Dynasty; the eight "Huangchao entering Chang'an"at the end of the Tang Dynasty; the ninth "the Humiliation of Jingkang" in North Song Dynasty; the tenth the destruction of the Song Dynasty by Mongolia. These ten are called "Ten Disasters."

An edition of *An Outline Treatise of Medical Herbs* (《本草纲目》), published in Japan at the turn of 17th century.

enlarging with the great enhancement of publishing strength. In 1950, there were 211 publishing houses in China and 12,153 kinds of books with the total printing runs of 275 million volumes in the same year. However, in 2007, there were 578 publishing houses and 248,283 kinds of books with the total runs of 6.293 billion volumes.

According to predictions in *A study on the system of development index of publishing industry in a well-off society* by the China Institute of Publishing Science, the added value of the Chinese publishing industry would reach RMB800 billion by 2020, accounting to 1.9–2.0% of GDP, and the types of books would be 300,000 with total press runs of 8.198 billion volumes.

Second, publishing technology is developing daily and digital publishing is booming. Combining computer technology with Chinese character printing, Chinese character laser photo-typesetting technique helps the Chinese printing industry end its history of lead and fire and step into a period of light and electricity. Meanwhile, featured by single volume as the minimal number and the goal to meet personalized requirements, printing on demand (POD) has become a new starting point. The development of digital technology is influencing the Chinese

Hand flatbed press, applied by Shanghai Newspaper Press (Shenbaoguan) in 1872.

publishing industry profoundly. Today's Chinese publishing market mainly consists of paper, online and mobile phone publication forms.

Third, the transition of commercialization in publishing system speeds up and the law system of publishing improves. The development of new technology and the Chinese market going global are changing the development model of Chinese publishing. Due to the changes taking place in the news and publishing, most publishing institutions are becoming modern companies consistent with the development of modern company culture.

In the field of circulation, publishing channels such as non-state-operated bookshops, online bookshops and reader clubs are rising. In the field of publishing educational research, higher education for and research on edition and publication in China have developed from nil and from small to large. With constant improvement of the legal system affecting the press and publications, the legal system framework centering on the Copyright Law has preliminarily taken shape and the

"Zhonghua Women" founded by Zhonghua Book Company. In the beginning stage of 20th century, the modern publishing in China presented an appearance of prosperity marked by the publishing of magazines in large scale.

law enforcement system for judicial and administrative protection has been formulated.

Fourth, the internationalization level is rising and copyright trade developing rapidly. After entering into the 21st century, China's publishing industry, with a constantly rising internationalization level and unceasing opening-up, has made remarkable achievements in copyright business and co-publishing. It not only actively introduces excellent books abroad, but also successfully releases many good publications on Chinese ancient civilization and contemporary culture. In the past ten years, the structure of copyright business in China has improved every year. The ratio of input to output was close to 5:1 in 2007 comparing to the 15:1 ten years ago. "Taking national culture as the mainstream, absorbing external valuable cultures to introduce Chinese culture to the world" the open layout of press and publishing is taking shape. Furthermore, Chinese publishers have frequently shown up in international book fairs including book fairs in Frankfurt, London and the US. The international impact of the yearly Beijing International Book Fair is progressively enhanced. What is worth mentioning is that the 2009 Frankfurt International Book

Fair, hailed as the most significant in the world, has seen China emerge as the main exhibitor and China displaying its splendid civilization of 5,000 years and narrating its profound changes with each passing day. With over 7,600 kinds of exhibits, there are numerous Chinese publishing houses at the fair consisting of 272 from Mainland China, 26 from Taiwan and 15 from Hong Kong. With more than 2,000 participants, China has copyright on 2,417 items. According to German official statistics, China is the main exhibitor and has drawn 290,000 visitors. It has effectively accelerated the development of Chinese publishing.

Since the 20th century, it is not only the publishing industry in the Chinese mainland that has expanded rapidly, but also the publishing industries in Chinese Taiwan, Hong Kong and Macao. Based on co-prosperity and development, the publishing industries in all these places create a pattern of diversity in unity of the Chinese publishing industry and play a positive role in the joint spread and inheritance of Chinese civilization. With a driving development trend that matches China's ancient publishing industry, they occupy a fundamental position in today's global publishing industry.

On the whole, the outstanding features of the Chinese publishing industry are rooted in the overall characteristics of Chinese culture and the progressive process of Chinese history. In a word, "classics in the past, innovation in the present." Its main features can be illustrated as follows:

(1) Time-honored history. From the perspective of historical inheritance, China, as one of the four ancient civilizations of the world, is also one of the early countries to start publishing activities. Since the literal invention and the documentary emergence, Chinese publishing activities have been evolving over 3,000 years.

(2) Rich content. The long-standing publishing activities preserve precious historical cultural heritage for today's

The numerous visitors in the "Classic and Innovation" pavilions in the China Section of the Frankfurt International Book Fair 2009

China and the world. In world history, Chinese works and old scriptures are huge in number, and there are plenty of carriers and book bindings. The development and revolution of printing technology, its extensive transmission, consistency and detailed extent, are worth earnest writing.

(3) **Unity in diversity.** "Diversity" means that the publishing industries from various ethnic groups have made glorious achievements besides the Han's; and "unity" indicates that the main content of various ethnic groups' publishing industries still show Chinese civilization consisting of Confucianism, Buddhism and Taoism. Nowadays, it presents itself as a Chinese-language publishing layout spanning the Straits, Hong Kong and Macao featuring unity in diversity, mutual benefit and harmonious development.

(4) **Profound influence.** China's publishing industry, which has shaped distinctive civilized pattern, not only deeply influences the formation and development of Chinese civilization, but also

significantly contributes to the development of the publishing industry in the world. Its outstanding embodiments are the extensive prevalence of papermaking and printing technology as well as the formation of a civilization zone in East Asia.

(5) Constant innovation. Making a general survey of the history of Chinese publishing, Chinese publishing activities at each phase have made new developments and become bigger, displaying a unique evolvement track and colorful development outlook. Chinese publishing culture boasts entrepreneurship and comprehensiveness, illustrated by independent innovation (papermaking and printing technology) and the absorption and fusion of external advanced cultures (Buddhism Introduction, the acceptance of western culture into China). Hence, it features prominent inclusiveness, which determines that Chinese publishing culture, having experienced thousands of years' of evolution, can be everlasting and achieve brilliant accomplishments.

This book mainly depicts the development skeleton and overall features of Chinese publishing, running through a remarkable history over 3,000 years in the making.

A Long-standing and Well-established History

The Origin and Development of China's Ancient Publishing Industry

The Xia Dynasty, established in 2070 B.C., was the first dynasty in China and marked the beginning of a new era in Chinese civilization. There is enough evidence to show that Chinese writing had been developed and was on its way to being systemized at the time. Besides, Chinese ancestors also developed a degree of aesthetics and cultural accomplishment. The appearance of primary writing tools and books paved the way for early publishing activities.

The Origin of Chinese Characters

The Chinese character is an important marker of humanity's shift from pre-literate to literate times. Written language is the basis of human civilization because it can be passed down through time and space. Chinese characters played a decisive role in the development of Chinese culture and the publishing industry.

The development of Chinese characters was a long process that can be divided into two periods before their real appearance. One is the time when the spoken language existed without a written one. The other is that of a written language without complete articles. On the basis of language and objectives, the real emergence of Chinese characters underwent three stages during which events were recorded by knotted cords, carvings and graphs.

Cangjie, a legendary figure in ancient China (2600 B.C.), claimed to be an official historian of the Yellow

Portrait of Cangjie

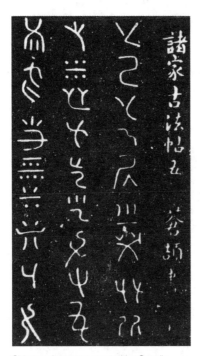

Chinese characters created by Cangjie according to the legend

Emperor and the inventor of the Chinese character. According to the legend he had four eyes to observe all things on earth. But that is only a legend. Historical records show Chinese characters had already been invented by Cangjie's time. By then, a certain number of characters were in use. Therefore, some scholars hold the view that Chinese characters had already been created but did not have any fixed style and that Cangjie's contribution was to unify and standardize them, which made later generations speak highly of him.

Knotting cords to record events, carved inscriptions, graphs and graphic symbols were the four important steps that led to the invention of the written language, according to historical documents and archaeological finds. Among these, graphic symbols or pictographic writing were most influential. Pictographic writing appeared in the later period of the primitive communes, namely the high days of the New Stone Age. Pictographic features can be found in many ethnic minority languages in China. A typical one is the Dongba Classics of the Naxi people in Yunnan Province. Dongba (the wizard) can read a lengthy poem from the Dongba Classics and tell vivid stories. Graphic symbols from the Classics were gradually developed into pictographic language.

Similar graphic symbols and writings are found among the

Dongba Classics

Yangshao culture of 4,000 B.C. and the Longshan Cultural Relics, which came later. Some 18 graphic symbols were found on the potteries of Ling Yanghe and Dazhu villages in Shandong Province. Four of them are pictured here:

Graphic symbols carved on the pottery founded in Dawenkou.

Many scholars consider these graphic symbols to be written language from the later period of the Dawenkou culture (about 2800–2500B.C.). Nevertheless, more and more archaeological discoveries prove that the Longshan Culture existed 4500 years ago. The period is also that of the Huangdi legend. It is around that time that Chinese characters essentially changed from rudimentary and began to take shape.

Archaeological finds show that writing tools existed before the invention of the written language. The Banpo pottery inscriptions have several designs similar to the human face, swimming fish

Pottery inscription of the Xia dynasty found in Erlitou, Henan Province

and the 米 pattern. They were drawn with writing brushes or other similar tools. The writings are clear and distinguishable. The pottery inscriptions found in Dawenkou, Shandong Province in 1959 include both carving and writing; which means that simple carving and writing tools were available at the time. The writing brush began to take on the features of a pen no later than during the Shang Dynasty.

With more expressive features, the carapace-bone-script emerged during the Shang Dynasty (1600–1046 B.C.) after a long evolution from the earliest characters. It is the earliest mature and systematic group of Chinese characters that can be seen today. After the oracle bone inscriptions, a variety of fonts, comprising bronze script, large seal script, small seal script, clerical script and regular script, appear throughout Chinese history. When it

A writing brush unearthed in Wuwei, Gansu Province. The writing brush was a basic writing tool in ancient China. It is still used by many people today.

The evolution of Chinese characters

comes to regular script, the grapheme—or smallest significant unit in a writing system—of Chinese characters, still in use today, was basically finalized.

Based on the premise of definite and clear meaning, the general evolution of Chinese characters is from complexity to simplicity. As a result, the pictographic characters originally used have been maintained ever since.

The Appearance of Books and Compilations

Written language is essential for books. When people developed a desire to spread or pass down their thoughts and experiences, they started to record their experiences and present their thoughts by consciously inscribing characters on various materials. It was then that books came into being.

Many scholars believe that classics and bibliographies emerged during the Xia Dynasty (2100–1600B.C.). This conclusion stems from multiple historical materials. *Shangshu*, the earliest history book ever found, says that records existed at the turn of the Xia

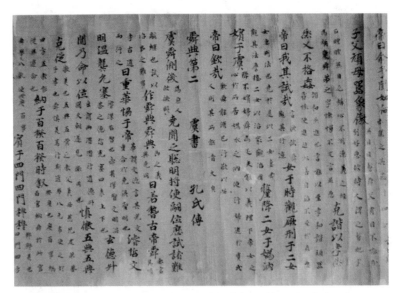

Shangshu in Tang dynasty (618–907), the earliest Chinese history book that shows books were in existence during the Xia Dynasty.

and Shang. According to *Lüshi Chunqiu*, another history book, during the Xia Dynasty there was not only a book ordinance but also an official Imperial Astronomer in charge of collecting and preserving books. *Lüshi Chunqiu* was once made public at the gate of Xianyang city for readers to edit. Gold rewards were promised to readers that could make improvements.

Without doubt, the documents and records of the Xia Dynasty are only writing records, or documentary archive material, rather than formal books. Nevertheless, they are the truthful records of people's activities with clear consciousness instead of rambling character presentations. They have some merit as books.

During the Shang Dynasty, ancient Chinese started writing on oracle bones, bronzes, jade, bamboo and wood to record information, which resulted in various types of document consisting of oracle bones inscriptions, bronze epigraphs, jade, bamboo and wooden slips. In terms of content, form and distribution, these inscriptions have qualities and features similar to books. These inscriptions already show some elements of compilation since some elements were developed during the process of renovating, writing, collecting and verifying, which can be regarded as the original editing activities before the emergence of formal books.

Governments started to establish special book collecting organizations during the Zhou Dynasty (1046–256 B.C.) when books truly emerged. After 770 B.C., feudal lords fought against one another while scholars gradually started writing more books. Confucius (551–479B.C.), the creator of Confucianism, edited and compiled many ancient classics

Xia Xiao Zheng, the calendar during the Xia Dynasty (2070–1600B. C.), still in use today, was recorded in this book.

Residual pages of the *Analects of Confucius* (the Tang Dynasty version), which truly recorded Confucius' thoughts.

and used them as textbooks in his teachings. Therefore Confucius may be considered China's first well-known book editor. Since then, the Chinese publishing industry has entered into a new development stage.

From Oracle Bone to Paper: Media of Ancient Books

With the invention of Chinese characters, a new problem emerged: What could be used to bear these characters to preserve and spread the knowledge they held? Pottery, bones, bronze, jade, bamboo and wood as well as silk were respectively used as books and record holders. After centuries of trial and error, papermaking was invented, which combined the merits of bamboo and wood slips with those of silk and overcame their deficiencies. Papermaking contributed tremendously to the history of publishing and the civilized history of the world.

Oracle bone

The most common writing material used by ancient Chinese was oracle bone made of tortoise shell and animal bones, especially ox scapula. Characters carved on these became known as oracle bone inscriptions. As an important medium for Chinese characters throughout the Xia and Shang dynasties, oracle bone inscriptions were very popular through the Yin Shang and Western Zhou dynasties (1046–711 B.C.).

Most of the oracle bones found to this day, mainly unearthed in the Yin ruins (Anyang city in Henan Province) and known as "the oracle bones of the Yin ruins," are the remnants from the mid and late Shang Dynasty (1300–1046 B.C.). The contents are mainly divination records from the Shang Dynasty. The Shang people were so superstitious that they enquired of God and their

Oracle bone inscriptions on tortoise shell

ancestors on virtually anything related to their lives. They were wont to seek divine guidance about hunting, farming, astronomical phenomena, harvest, war, disease and sacrifices. As a result, most of oracle bones included divination records from the time. In addition, there were a number of inscriptions to record important data such as the number of prisoners of war, the number of hunted animals, rewards and sacrifices. In general, the records found in oracle bones touch upon various aspects of social life from the time.

The oracle bones are essentially a type of written record. In terms of their content and binding, these oracle bones already have some elements of books.

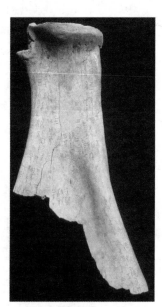

Oracle bones with inscriptions made up of relatively mature Chinese characters.

Bronze wares

Bronze is an alloy of brass and tin. Utensils made by bronze are called bronze wares. Inscriptions carved on bronze wares are called epigraphs or bronze inscriptions. During the Xia and Shang dynasties, a great number of bronze works were produced. The Western Zhou Dynasty (1600–771 B.C.) was the golden age of bronze.

With various styles and fine designs, bronze works can be classified as daily wares and musical instruments. When they started to be used as vessels in sacrificial ceremonies, bronze works, an authoritative emblem became "a treasure" for building and consolidating state power. Due to such special recognition, the aristocracy would cast a piece of bronze and

The "Great Ding" (tripod), made in the early Shang Dynasty, unearthed in Shang Cheng, Zhengzhou City.

"Ligui" (a bronze altar made in the Western Zhou Period) bears the inscription of King Wu of Zhou, who annihilated the Shang Dynasty.

Bronze inscription on the Maogong Ding (tripod) and its rubbings

use it to inscribe important data or event records, all information that needed to be preserved for a long time and permanently remembered. Therefore, the characters inscribed on bronze wares are called inscriptions.

To date, tens of thousands of bibliography inscriptions from the Shang to the Han Dynasty (206 B.C.–220 A.D.) have been found in China. Not a few of them are long passages among which the longest existing bronze inscription is the one on the Maogong Ding (tripod) with 497 words. The main contents of bronze inscriptions include records of sacrificial ceremonies, war, largess, government documents, emperor's speeches and tributes to ancestors. These are more abundant than Oracle bone inscriptions.

Compared with oracle bone inscriptions, bronze inscriptions have more space and more versatile, some were consciously made for reading. With more range, the bronze inscriptions are more like books in their function.

Stone inscription

Ancient people used to carve chronicle scripts on stones that could be more easily found, kept and made than metals. Stone inscriptions could be easily publicized and showed. During the

Stone Classics of the Xiping Reign
The engraving of Stone Classics of the Xiping Reign, lasting 9 years ranging from 175–183A.D., presided over by the noted scholar Cai Yong. There were 46 stone monuments for 7 Confucian classics: *I Ching, Poems of Lu State, The Book of History, The Spring and Autumn Annals, The Biography of Gongyang, Ceremonies and Rituals and Analects of Confucius*, which started engraving in the Xiping Reign and gained the name as Stone Classics of the Xiping Reign. The stone classics, stood in front of the gate of Imperial College in Luoyang, the capital at the time, attracted numerous people to watch and copy every day. As the earliest Confucian officially-definitive edition of classics in Chinese history, the stone classics is not only a massive governmental proofread for Confucian classics, but also an editing and publishing especially one run on a large scale by government, which, to a certain degree, facilitated the emergence of beating-rubbing technique and the invention of printing technology.

Spring and Autumn Period (770–476 B.C.), there were records of stone inscriptions.

The earliest stone inscriptions in existence in China are stone scripts in the shape of a drum from the Spring and Autumn period. Ten pieces of inscribed stones shaped like drums were unearthed in Fengxiang County, Shaanxi Province during the early Tang dynasty. The inscribed characters with a font somewhere between bronze inscription and small official script were verses about hunting—they are called "Hunting Tablets."

Emperor Qin Shihuang (259–210 B.C.) popularized stone inscriptions by using them in various places to make his efforts to unite the country known as he undertook inspection tours throughout his 12-year reign. During the Eastern Han Dynasty (25–220 A.D.), stone carvings became very popular. There were many great articles engraved on stone, among which the most famous one was "Xiping Stone Classics." It launched the history of engraving ancient Confucian classics, playing significant role in the development of books. After that, the imitators in the later generations followed suit. The result was a six-fold increase in inscribing activities. Of the resulting products, only the "Kaicheng Stone Classics of the Tang Dynasty" (now kept in the Forest of Steles in Xi'an) and the "Qianlong Stone

Stone drum and its rubbings

Classics of the Qing Dynasty" (now kept in the Imperial Academy in Beijing) have been completely preserved.

The rubbings of Mt. Yi Stone Inscription by Qin Shihuang (the first emperor of Qin Dynasty)

Besides the Confucian classics, Buddhist and Taoist classics from various dynasties were also engraved on stone. The most splendid were the Buddhist stone inscriptions in Mt. Shijing in Fangshan District, Beijing. A total of 3,572 volumes of 1,122 Buddhist classics were engraved on the 14,278 stone sheets from the early 7th century to 12th century. These stone inscriptions were called "Tripitaka of Yunju Temple in Fangshan" or "Fangshan stone inscriptions."

Kaicheng Stone Classics from the Tang dynasty (now kept in the Forest of Steles in Xi'an).

Bamboo and wooden slips

Before the invention of papermaking, polished bamboo and wood slips were the earliest, most widely used and the most influential writing materials. A single bamboo slip was called *Jian* while numerous bamboo slips linked together were *Ce;* or *"Jian Ce."* Blank wooden slips were called *Ban* while written ones were *Du.* Slender wooden slips were called *Mu Jian* and wooden slips were *Ban Du* while the bamboo ones were *Jian Du.*

In terms of time, bamboo and wood as a writing material can be traced back to the 21st century B.C. or before, even before the use of oracle bones, metal and stone.

In terms of content, bamboo and wooden slips can be classified into clerical documents and books which included Confucian classics, history and geography books, laws and regulations, military books and chronicles. Compared with oracle bones,

 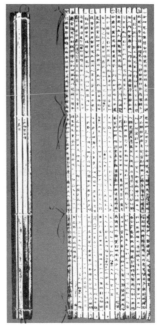

The thin wood script of weapons in the West Han Dynasty, unearthed in Juyan

Wuwei bamboo and wood slips from the Han Dynasty

stones and metal, bamboo and wood have their own merits. They are of low cost and easily found. It is easy to make slips that are good for writing and amending. Moreover, the slips can be linked into volumes to better spread of culture. As a result, along with silk and paper, bamboo and wood slips were used as writing material for hundreds of years even after paper was invented. They did not exit as viable writing materials until the end of the Eastern Jin Dynasty (317–420) in the 4th century.

Silk manuscripts

Silk manuscripts or textile writing, are characters written on various kinds of silk. The silk culture, which originated in China, was recognized around the globe. According to ancient books, silk began to be used as a writing material no later than the Spring and Autumn Period and prevailed for about 700–800 years throughout the Warring States and Three Kingdoms Period (220–280).

The real silk manuscript, unearthed in the Chu tomb of Changsha in 1934, was called "the Chu Silk Manuscript." It includes written content about many important legendary figures surrounded by colored mysterious images in Chinese ink and done with writing brushes. This is the earliest silk manuscript ever found and maintained to date.

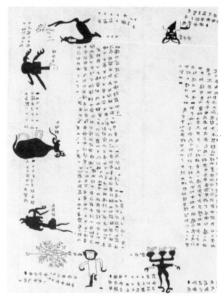

Part of "the Chu silk manuscripts" of Warring States Period.

The most silk manuscripts were unearthed in Mawangdui Han tombs in Changsha. In 1973, more than 120,000 words in 20 kinds of books were found, like *Lao Zi* (two

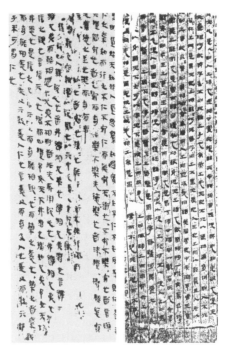

Silk copy of the *Strategies of the Warring States*.

Version A and Version B of silk manuscripts of *Lao Zi*

versions), *I Ching, Intrigues of the Warring States* and *Strategies of the Warring States*. Silk was used not only in writing but drawing, including diagrams and maps in bamboo and wooden slips. There were *Dao Yin Tu* and other three ancient maps in the Mawangdui Silk Texts.

The merits of silk for writing were that the silk, not as heavy and clumsy as bamboo and wood slips, could be easily cut into different sizes and was convenient. It had a large capacity but required little space, for writing, keeping, carrying and reading. However, due to its higher cost, silk used in writing was far beyond the reach of ordinary people. The biggest merit of silk manuscripts was that it enlightened people to produce a new writing material that was easier

Painting on silk from
Tomb 1 of Mawangdui.

to write on and inexpensive. After years of exploration and practice, Chinese ancestors finally invented papermaking on the basis of silk rinsing and retting techniques.

Papermaking technique

As one of the four great inventions of ancient China—along with printing, gunpowder and the compass—papermaking was an amazing achievement of ancient Chinese science and technology.

Numerous archeological findings show that ancient Chinese invented plant fiber paper during the Western Han Dynasty based on long-time productive practice. Paper was made during the Western Han Dynasty during every emperor's regime and the years' ranging from Wendi Emperor (180–157 B.C.) to the Xinmang Period (9–23 A.D.), has been unearthed. In 1986, ancient paper from 176–141 B.C. yellow, thin and soft with maps on it was unearthed in Fangmatan Han Tombs in Tianshui, Gansu Province. Gray and yellow paper with

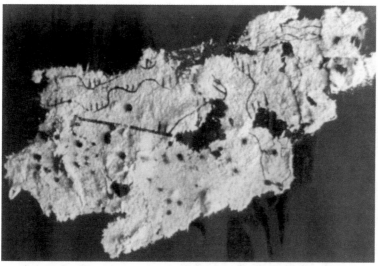

Ancient paper with a map (from around 176–141 B.C. unearthed in Fangmatan, Gansu Province, 1986)

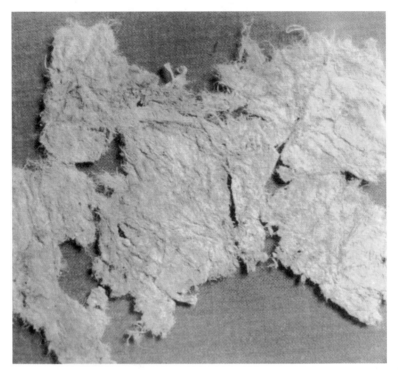

Pieces of ancient paper (unearthed in Majuanwan, Dunhuang, 1979)

50 words in 7 lines (written around 89–97 A.D.) was found in the Chake'ertie Hanfengsui Relic in the eastern bank of E'jina River, Gansu Province in 1942. The pale-yellow ancient paper, discovered in Tianshuijin Hanxuanquan Youyi Relic in Dunhuang, Gansu Province, was of refined texture with written words around 8–23 A.D. The discovery of the large quantity of Western Han paper proves that plant fiber paper existed in China in the 2nd century B.C.

The invention of plant fiber paper, which was convenient, inexpensive, light, soft and enduring, fundamentally changed the media used to record and spread knowledge and significantly promoted the publishing industry and society's progress.

The restorative processes of papermaking. (No.1, 3: Washing. No. 2:
Cutting. No.4: Making plant ash water. No.5: Steaming and boiling. No.6: Ramming.
No.7: Routing. No.8: Paper making. No.9: Drying and releasing.)

During the Eastern Han Dynasty, Cai Lun (about 63–121 A.D.) having innovated papermaking, presented the emperor with paper he made in 105 A.D., earning high praise. From then on, this kind of paper grew in popularity across the country and became known as "Caihou Paper," named after the inventor. After that, paper, with the gradual improved technique and ever-lower costs, evolved as the most universal writing material of the time. Not until the 4th century A.D. did paper replace bamboo, wood slips, as well as silk and became the popular writing material of society.

The Evolution of Publishing

Marked with papermaking and printing techniques, the history of Chinese publishing can be divided into four stages: The bamboo inscription and silk manuscripts period from the establishment of Xia Dynasty (21st century B.C.) to the 2nd century B.C. (before the invention of papermaking); the manuscript book period from the 1st century B.C. to the 7th century A.D. (before the invention of printing); the manual printing period from the 7th century A.D. to 1840s (before the western printing machines came to China); and the mechanical printing period from 1840s to the early 1900s.

Since the 20th century, Chinese publishing has officially entered the modern publishing period and has kept step with the growth trends of global publishing.

Relics of bamboo and wood slips from the Han Dynasty, found in Juyan, Gansu Province.

Bamboo inscription and silk manuscripts period (2100–200 B.C.)

During the period, Chinese publishing activities

gradually became more mature and made a rapid progress in the type of writing materials used, compiling, copying and forming. With a bright feature of the times, Chinese publishing ultimately became a historical activity of developed its own systems.

In this period, the early evolution, Chinese characters, oracle bones, bronze inscriptions, seal scripts and clerical script phases, enormously strengthened the convenience of writing. Among the widely used writing materials such as bamboo and wood, oracle bones, bronze and stone as well as silk, bamboo and wood were used for a long time across the country and resulted in the early book form of bamboo and wood slips.

The number and length of Chinese books increased a lot as academic culture and the carriers of language developed. Books that could represent the essence of Chinese culture were written, such as the *Classic of Changes*, *The Book of Poetry*, *Analects of Confucius*, *Lao Zi*, *Art of War of Sun Zi* and *Records of the Grand Historian*. These, each thousands or tens of thousands words long, were written on bamboo and wood slips to hand down to generations.

Book collection activities were gradually expanded and the collection of books in government book agencies grew. Through a combination of compiling, arranging, writing, and classical collecting, government book agencies further perfected their function to act as government publishing agencies. A large quantity of government publications were published and distributed.

At the same time, academic development increased people's need for books. Confucianism was honored as the national classics of the Han Dynasty, which excited society's passion to pursue it. Soon after books appeared they began to spread. By means of transcription, borrowing and teaching, books became widespread.

Meanwhile, book transcribing became a special occupation and the trade evolved. With the bloom of the book business, Shusi, the earliest bookstore in Chinese history came into being in the capital city of Chang'an and other economically and culturally developed cities at the end of the 2nd century B.C.

China had had economic and cultural communication with its neighboring countries since the 3rd century B.C. At the time Buddhism and the classics were introduced into China and had a great influence on Chinese society.

Through long exploration, papermaking was invented in China in the 2nd century B.C. After that, paper, as well as bamboo and wood slips, was used as writing material. Not until the early 5th century did paper, by order of the emperor, totally replace bamboo and wood slips and became popular.

Manuscript book period (200 B.C.–700 A.D.)

It was in this period that the Chinese publishing industry went into its early golden days. The initial stage of the manuscript book period lasted from the 2nd century B.C. to the 4th century A.D. During this stage, bamboo and wood slips, silk and paper were used as writing material in parallel. Its main stage was the 5th to the 7th century A.D, which was also its peak time. After the 8th century, with the extensive application of printing, manuscript books co-existed with printed books for quite a long period. Then printed books became the mainstream. The history of manuscript books is more than one thousand years old.

After paper became popular thanks to constant improvements and development, a system of books, called a scroll system, was shaped from transcription to scroll making.

In that period, the number and kinds of books increased significantly. Rough statistics show that about 11,754 works made up of 73,200 scrolls were produced from 25 A.D. to 618

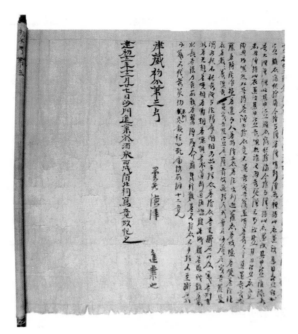

The 416 A.D. Buddhist Scriptures Manuscript. An early scrolls found in Dunhuang's Grottoes of Buddhist Texts of Gansu Province.

A.D, which included general encyclopedia, collected works, rhyme dictionaries, genealogies and other types of books. The translation of Buddhist scriptures boomed in this period and about 1,500 works on 4,000 strolls were translated from 220 A.D. to 618 A.D. The translation level substantially improved. At the same time, with the widespread use of paper, the space and number of words in a single work increased in quantity, works with hundreds of thousands of words were quite common at the time.

With the increasing number and types of books, arranging and cataloguing emerged. During 26–6 B.C., Liu Xiang, with the emperor's support, organized scholars to create a systematic arrangement for the country's national book collection. With 13,269 books organized, it was the first large-scale book arrangement by the state. In the process, Liu Xiang and others wrote a bibliography for each book and edited the first systematic book catalogue in ancient China.

The books were classified into six categories: "Six Classical Arts" referred to Confucianism classical works and reading materials for the "Six Meridians," "The philosophers" to selected readings of Confucian and other ancient Chinese classics since Pre-Qin Days; "Poetry" to Poems; "Han Odes" to literary output; "Military Book" to military works; "Shushu" and "Fangji" to works about natural and applied science. These are the well-known "Six Classifications" in Chinese history.

After that, there were activities to arrange the national collection of books and compiling a library catalogue in successive dynasties. Progress, however, lead to great changes in the classification of books. In 636 A.D, *Sui Shu*, an official history book created by Wei Zheng and others included a "Bibliography of Chronicles" that recorded 3,127 collected books comprising of 36,708 volumes, and 1,064 lost books consisting of 12,759 volumes. Based on the previous book classification system, the recorded books were catalogued into four sections: Jing, Shi, Zi and Ji. Just as the names implied that "Jing" referred to Confucian classics works; "Shi" to various types of history books; "Zi" to readings of Confucian and other ancient Chinese classics as well as Buddhism, Taoism and other religious works; and "Ji" to literature works. This is the famous "Four Classifications" in ancient China, which had over 40 minor catalogues. In addition, there were Taoist scriptures and Buddhist scriptures attached.

The *Bibliography of Chronicles of the Sui Dynasty*, to certain degree, reflects the profile and structure of Chinese books in the manuscript book period and then the cultural features as well as the structure of the traditional academy. It had a significant impact on book classification in later generations. The library catalogue afterwards was established on that base. To this day,

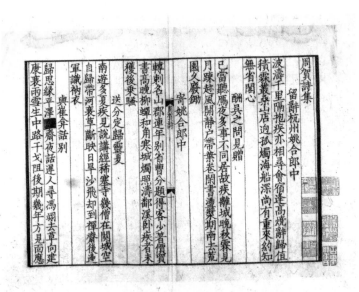

Zhou He's Poems published by Chens Bookstore in Lin'an during the Southern Song Dynasty in Hangzhou, a representative product of workshop printing.

the "Four Classification" is still employed in arranging and cataloguing ancient books in many places in China.

The major duplicating method in this period was transcription. As books became well known and people sought them out, the book trade became a growing business. There were numerous transcribers who earned their livelihoods by transcribing books. Transcribing was a profession at the time. With the spread of papers and improvements in ink-making, unprecedented progress was made in duplicating techniques. Moreover, the invention of stamping and watercolor sealing techniques provided technical possibilities for the invention of printing technique while traditional transcribing was very popular.

Meanwhile, Chinese books and papermaking began to spread to Vietnam, Korea, Japan and other neighboring countries, greatly impacting the development of publishing in those countries.

Manual printing period (the 7th century A.D.–1840s)

From 700 to the 1840s, Chinese printing was stuck in block printing. The period is called "Manual Printing Period." The Chinese publishing industry rose to its highest splendor during this period. Not later than the 7th century A.D, engraving, typography and registration printing were invented in China. These inventions marked a new stage in Chinese publishing that led to rapid progress in the quality and quantity of books. From then on, the Chinese publishing industry became increasingly more popular and soon developed into five systems, which were: government printing, private printing, workshop printing, temple printing and college printing. All these systems mutually influenced and stimulated one another in their development.

1597 (Wanli 25th year) version of *Story of Pipa* of the Ming Dynasty, at the time, preprints of dramas and novels were very popular.

A carved copy of the *Original Meaning of I Ching of the* Changes of the Qing dynasty by the inner court in the reign of Emperor Kangxi

The government and private printing systems, with a rapid increase in the number of books published, went into an era of unprecedented prosperity. More than 14,000 works in 218,029 volumes were published during the Ming dynasty, some of which were huge classic works like *Yongle Encyclopedia* and *Siku Quanshu*.

A large quantity of huge classics, like Confucian classics, historical classics and Tripitaka, were inscribed many times. Each copy represented a significant publishing event, which showed the publishing capability during the manual printing period of ancient China.

As the production capacity grew, official and private book collections were enlarged and book collecting and protecting experience accumulated. There were many famous libraries like the Huang Shi Cheng Library and the Tian Yi Library. At the same time, not only government organizations and schools engaged in book publishing and selling, but civil book workshops undertook a more vigorous trade. In the big publishing centers around the country, there were countless book workshops. The publishing industry, with the new phenomenon like the emergence of book advertisements and copyright protection, developed as a commodity economy.

To meet the development needs of the printing industry, ancient Chinese books gradually evolved into album binding forms consisting of folding forms, butterfly-like binding, wrapped-ridge binding and thread binding and finalized the design of thread-binding form.

In this period, book circulation and trade expanded further, flourishing exceptionally. Not only government organizations and schools engaged in book publishing and selling, but also civil book workshops undertook more vigorous trade. Exchanges of publications between China and foreign counties expanded so that lots of Chinese books were exported. Papermaking and printing spread across Asia and Europe, which deeply influenced world publishing. At the end of 16th century, western missionaries started their translations and writings in China, which brought a new air to the publishing and cultural circles.

However, in the 19th century, Chinese publishing still could not break away from manual printing and could not bring about capitalist management without a breakthrough in book content and format. As a result, Chinese publishing was left behind. After the Opium War in 1840, traditional Chinese society gradually collapsed and stepped towards modernization. With the introduction of modern western publishing techniques, a fundamental revolution took placed in Chinese publishing.

From then on, Chinese publishing went into the machine-printing period. At the turn of 20th century, many private publishing houses, like the Commercial Press and the Zhonghua Book Company, were established. China's publishing industry finally emerged from its backward condition and began to open a new chapter of modern publication. As to the modern Chinese publishing industry, that is best left to another chapter.

Classical Ancient Books
The Workmanship of Ancient Chinese Books

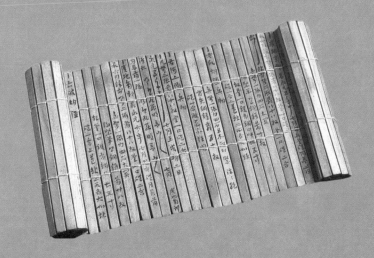

Selected Content and Editing Format of Ancient Books

In general, the editing format of ancient Chinese books can be divided into two kinds. One is co-editing presided by the government. Many books, such as *Yongle Encyclopedia*, *Siku Quanshu* and others are co-compiled. The other is individual editing by the author or editor. Likewise, numerous books are individually-compiled like *The Records of the Grand Historian*, *The Articles of the Whole Ancient Times,Three Generations,Qin and Han Dynasty,the Three Kingdoms and Six Dynasties* and others. A well-established routine and profuse editing consideration by generations of editors has exerted a far-reaching impact on later editing work.

The substance of ancient Chinese books is not only wide in scope but also continuously enriched and updated with the progress of time. The results are easily visible the following statistical table for ancient Chinese works by Wang Yuguang.

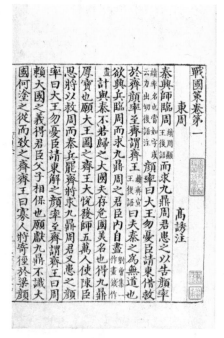

Xueyan Study's handwritten copy of *The Warring States Scheme* from the Ming Dynasty, which was sorted out and named by Liuxiang and others.

Statistical table for ancient Chinese works

Dynasty	Year	Total number of works	Total Volumes	Average number of works per century	Growth rate
West Han Dynasty and before (before 25 B.C.)	747	1,033	13,029	138	
Eastern Han Dynasty (25–220)	195	1,100	2,900	564	309%
Wei, Jin, Southern and Northern & Sui dynasties (220–618)	398	10,654	70,304	2,679	375%
Tang and Five Dynasties Period (618–960)	342	10,806	185,074	3,160	18%
Song Dynasty (960–1279)	319	11,519	124,919	3,611	14%
Western Xia, Liao, Jin & Yuan dynasties (906–1368)	462	5,970	52,891	1,292	–64%
Ming Dynasty (1368–1644)	276	14,024	218,029	5,081	293%
Qing Dynasty (1616–1911)	295	126,649	1,700,000	42,932	745%
The period before Anti-Japanese War in the reign of the Republic of China (1912–1937)	25	71,680	91,378	286,720	568%

Bibliographies of ancient Chinese books compiled by the past dynasties offer a sound reflection of the substance of the works.

Formal, large-scale proofreading and cataloguing in ancient China started during the Western Han Dynasty. At the end of the Western Han Dynasty, noted scholars Liu Xiang and Liu Xin (father and son) were tasked with systemizing the state book collection. The father and son team classified the books into six categories based on existing academic categories and bibliographies. The bibliography of *The Han Dynasty · Bolographic Treatise* roughly illustrates the classifications the father and son used. It is outlined below.

Outline—Preface

Six classical arts—9 types, namely, *Yi, Shu, Shi, Li, Yue, Chunqiu, Lunyu, Xiaojing* and *Xiaoxue*; recorded books by 129 scholars, 2,926 articles and 1 scroll of pictures.

Various Schools of thought and their exponents—10 types namely, Confucian, Dao, Yinyang, Fa, Ming, Mencius, Zongheng, Za, Nong and Xiaoshuo; recorded books by 187 scholars, 4,346 articles.

Poems—20 Quyuan-like scholars, 21 Lujia-like scholars, 25 Sunqing-like scholars, 5 types of Za Fu and Sing poetry; recorded books by 106 scholars, 1,313 articles.

Military—4 types of *Quanmou, Xingshi, Yinyang* and *Jiqiao*; recorded books by 66 scholars, 1,375 articles,44 scrolls of pictures.

Mathematics—6 types of astronomy, *Lipu, Wuxing, Zhugui, Zazhan* and *Xingfa*; recorded books by 110 scholars, 2,557 articles.

Science—4 types of *Yijing, Jingfang, Fangzhong* and *Shenxian*; recorded books by 36 scholars, 862 articles.

In total, there were records for 13,397 books in 38 types and 6 categories, written by 634 scholars and 45 scrolls of pictures.

The Six Classical Arts refers to Confucian classic works and basic readings on the "six meridians." Among the most significant are "Paying Supreme Tribute to Confucianism" in the Han Dynasty; "The philosophers outside the Confucians" the selected readings of

Portrait of Ji Yun, chief-editor of *Siku Quanshu*

Confucius and other ancient Chinese classics in pre-Qin Days. "Sing poetry" refers to the poetry just as the name implies, which was a popular style during the Han Dynasty, which led to it being singled out as a specific category. "Military" works, which were very effective in consolidating the feudal regime an age of frequent war. There were many books of this kind in the Period of Spring and Autumn and Warring States," so it ranked above "Mathematics" and "Science." The "Mathematics" and "Science" categories mainly refer to the works about natural and applied science. "Outline" means "the compendium of six categories" or "the compendium of all books," which explains the significance of the six categories and their academic origins, elaborates on the interrelation and application of the six categories and, because it is equal to the total order of the book, it ranks above the six categories. The book classification roughly corresponds to the contents and academic development before the Western Han Dynasty.

After the Han Dynasty, the book classification changed according to the development of China's publishing industry. In the early Tang Dynasty, the *Bibliography of Chronicles of the Sui Dynasty*, by Wei Zheng (580–643) and others, adopted "Four Classifications" of "*Jing, Shi, Zi* and *Ji*" with a supplement containing Taoist scriptures and Buddhist scriptures. In addition, there were 40 minor-catalogues: below the Four Categories: 10"*Jing*" catalogues, 13 "*Shi*" catalogues, 14 "*Zi*" catalogues, 3 "*Ji*" catalogues, 4 "*Tao*" and 11 "*Budha*" catalogues. Their specific lists were as follows:

"*Jing*": *Yi, Shu, Shi, Li, Yue, Chunqiu, Lunyu, Xiaojing, Chenwei Shu* and *Xiaoxue*

"*Shi*": *Zhengshi, Gushi, Zashi, Bashi, Qijuzhu, Jiushi, Zhiguan, Yizhu, Xingfa, Zazhuan, Dili, Puxi* and *Bulu.*

"*Zi*": *Confucianism, Dao, Fa, Ming, Mo, Zongheng, Za, Nong, Xiaoshuo, Bing,* astronomy, *Lisu, Wuxing,* and *Yifang.*

"Ji": Chuci, Bieji and *Zongji.*

"Supplement": Taoist scriptures and Buddhist scriptures.

The book classifications offer a rough reflection of the book publication and academic development before the Tang Dynasty. The "Four Classifications" system in *Bibliography of Chronicles of the Sui Dynasty* exerted a tremendous influence on later book categories, the typical one of which, which is alos the most comprehensive, abundant and influential, is *General Catalogue of Four Treasuries.*

The *General Catalogue of Siku Quanshus,* also called the *General Index of the Complete Works of the Siku Quanshu,* was linked to the compiling of *Siku Quanshu* during the Qing Dynasty, which is the summary, written by the editors, finalized by the chief editor Jiyun (who also called himself Xiaolan, 1724–1805) and authorized by the Emperor, to include the content, the dynasty of writing, the writer's biography and the original version of the books. The book records 3,461 kinds of ancient works in 79,309 volumes in *Siku Quanshu,* and 6,793 kinds in 93,550 volumes not included in *Siku Quanshu,* which basically includes ancient Chinese works before the Period of Emperor Qianlong of the Qing Dynasty. With 200 volumes, the book can be divided into 4 classifications, 44 categories and 66 minor-catalogues.

"Jing": Yi, Shu, Shi, Li, Chunqiu, Xiaojing, Wujing, Sishu, Yue and *Xiaoxue* in 10 minor-catalogues.

"Shi": Zhengshi, Biannianshi, Jishibenmoshi, Zashi, Bieshi, Zhaolingzhouyi, Zhuanji, Shichao, Zaiji, Shiling, Dili, Zhiguan, Zhengshu, Mulu and *Shiping* in 15 minor-catalogues.

"Zi": Confucianism, *Bingjia, Fajia, Nongjia, Shijia,* astronomy, *Shushu, Yishu, Pulu, Zajia, Leishu, Xiaoshuojia, Yijia* and *Daojia* in 14 minor-catalogues.

"Ji": Chuci, Bieji, Zongji, Shiwenping and *Ciqu* in 5 minor-catalogues.

The *General Catalogue of Siku Quanshu,* featuring a complete collection of traditional book-cataloguing with a total order for each category, a short preface for each catalogue and an abstract for each book, is an agglomeration of the Four Classifications in ancient books. With a huge space, a comprehensive institution and abundant substance, it is a summary for the academy in China before the 18th century and has a certain academic value.

Printing and Transcription: Reproduction of Ancient Publications

The invention of movable-type print is a significant event in the development of human society, which has greatly sped up the development of culture around the world. As the first country to invent movable-type print, printing technique in ancient China included three distinct types: block-printing, movable-type printing and registration printing, of which block-printing was the earliest and most popular. Following the invention of movable-type printing, China's printing industry bloomed but the tradition of transcription remained, giving the new period of printing a traditional flavor.

Engraving printing

Engraving printing was also called whole-page printing or block printing. Pear wood or Chinese jujube tree wood was usually used to make a block, and then thin paper with characters

Tools used in engraving printing

written in reverse (a mirror-image) was stuck on the surface of the block. At this moment it was only necessary to ink the base slab and bring it into contact with the paper or cloth to achieve an acceptable print. In ancient times, this technique was called woodblock printing because people pressed the paper on the surface of the prepared and inked woodblock. Based on current evidence, printing technique was invented in China, not later than between the 7th and the 8th century (during the early and the glorious period of the Tang Dynasty) and most likely at the turn of the 7th century A.D.

In the existing documents from Tang Dynasty, there are many records that describe the invention and the application of printing during the Tang Dynasty. In the preface of Bai Juyi's (779–831) *Chang Qing Collection* (《长庆集》) in the 4th year of Emperor Tang Mu, poet Yuan Zhen wrote that Bai Juyi and Yuan Zhen's poems were published in quantities, sold in bookstores and widely read. In 835, the government banned private printing because private publishing workshops printed a huge number of calendars. All these prove that block printing was widely used

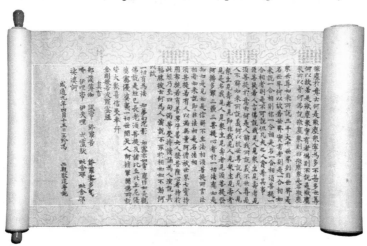

The printed copy of *Diamond Sutra* from the Tang Dynasty in 868

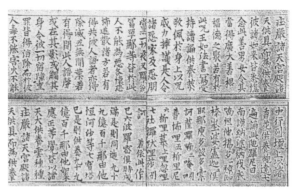

Pure Light Dharani Sutra unearthed in South Korea

in the 9th century; so it is possible to infer that block printing was invented earlier.

All existing early prints were made during the Tang Dynasty. The two best-known examples are *Diamond Sutra*, unearthed in Dunhuang, China in 868. This is the earliest wood block print in existence. The *Diamond Sutra* is a complete scroll with simple but heavy-colored illustrations, delicate painting, skilled cutting, even ink and clear printing. It was apparently made with a

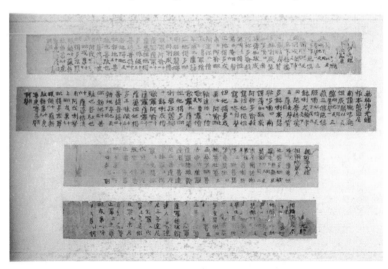

Pure *Light Dharani Sutra* unearthed in Japan (Million Sutra)

mature technique and is definitely not the output early stage printing.

The other is the Chinese character print from Empress Wu Zetian's period (690–705) of the Tang Dynasty. It was unearthed from Korea and Japan in 20th century. It inclues the *Pure Light Dharani Sutra* unearthed in Sarira pagoda in the Pulguksa Temple, Gyeongju, Korea and the Million Sutra made before 770 A.D. under the command of Empress Shotoku. It was kept in Horyuji in Yamatoji, Japan and the London museum.

All these findings in Korea and Japan show that Chinese woodblock printing developed at a relatively higher level and the quality and scale was good enough for international spread.

Movable-type printing

Movable-type printing is a system of printing and typography that uses movable components to reproduce the elements of a document (usually individual characters or punctuation) by making single tablets in lines. Tablets can be separated after use and rearranged for another printing.

Bi Sheng (?–1051) invented ceramic movable type, the earliest movable type known, during the Northern Song Dynasty (960–1127). The invention is described in detail in *Dream Pool Essays* (《梦溪笔谈》) by Shen Kuo (1031–1095), from which learn about the production method of movable type and the process of movable-type printing.

After Bi Sheng's death, movable type was obtained by Shen Kuo's

Portrait of Bi Sheng

The restored graph of the wheel of the composing frame invented by Wang Zhen

later generations, and was still used until the book *Dream Pool Essays* was written. This proves the reliability and authority of the book. Afterwards, Bi Sheng's successors continued to use movable-type printing in later generations.

During the early Yuan Dynasty (1206–1368), the known agronomist Wang Zhen made significant innovations on wooden movable type printing. In 1298, Wang Zhen applied wooden movable type printing, to produce 100 copies of the *Records of Jingde County* in s single month by himself. The *Records of Jingde County* has mover than 60 thousand words. In addition, Wang wrote about his experience in an article named *Ways to Make Types and Print Books* to preserve the historical process. He also invented the wheel of the composing frame with movable type characters arranged primarily through a rhyming scheme. Workers could pick up tablets by rotating the wheel while sitting.

Wooden movable type printing spread to minority group areas and was used to print their books during the Yuan dynasty. Hundreds of wooden movable types in the Uighur language were found in thousands of Buddhism caves in Dunhuang, Gansu Province.

The printing of *Wu Ying Dian Ju Zhen Ban Collections* in 1773,

The wooden movable type with Uighur script, the earliest alphabetic writing from the early 13th century, unearthed in Dun Huang caves.

with 134 kinds in more than 2,300 volumes, was the largest scale wooden movable type printing effort of the Qing Dynasty. Jin Jian who took charge of the edition recorded his printing experience in *Wu Ying Dian Selective Collections*, which was an important record of China's publishing history and was translated into German, English and other languages.

Ancient Chinese metal movable type included bronze, tin and lead type, in which hand made bronze type was used first and most. Bronze type printing flourished at the end of fifteenth

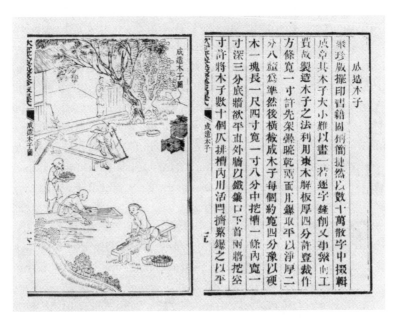

The illustration of Working Processes of *Wu Ying Dian Selective Collections*, a wooden movable type copy from the Qian Long period of the Qing Dynasty.

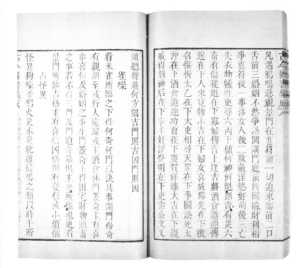

A copy printed with bronze movable-type of *The Compendium of Works of Past and Present* from the Qing Dynasty.

century. The best-known examples come from rich families known as Huasui, Huajian and Anguo who printed books with bronze type in Wuxi of Jiangsu.

The most famous bronze movable-type print was the inner court of *The Compendium of Works of Past and Present* in Qing Dynasty. From the 4th to 6th year of Yongzheng Period (1726–1728), the Qing government printed 65 copies with 5,200 volumes each in large and small fonts. This was an unprecedented printing effort with the largest word count and exquisite typography.

Color woodcut printing

Color woodcut printing was based on woodblock printing, which can successively print several colors on the same piece of paper by using different sizes of blocks with different colors. Books printed with this technique are called registration editions.

Early in the use of this technique, the most common colors used were red and black—these books are called "Prints in red and black" or "Mackle prints," afterwards, with four or five

Notes to Wuwen Monk Diamond Sutra carved by Zifu Temple in the early years of the Yuan Dynasty (1340)

colors involved, the overprinted books became known as "Four-color prints" or "Five-color prints" according to the number of colors involved.

Based on archeological discoveries, color woodcut printing was invented, closely following the invention xylography, during the Period of Song, Liao and Jin dynasties (960–1234). In the extant real objects, there are three color-overprinted "Nama Sakyamuni Buddha," with the printing time estimated to be during the Tonghe Period in the Liao Dynasty (982–1012), found in Fogong Temple, Yingxian County, Shanxi Province; and the *Notes to Wuwen Monk Diamond Sutra* engraved in 1340 with two colors: red as the text and black as notes, as well as a red-black illustrations of

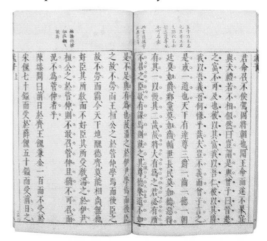

Min's version of three-color overprint of *Notes and Commentary of the Three Classics* during the Wanli Period of the Ming Dynasty

The four-color overprint of the *Guwen Yuanjian* in the Kangxi Period of the Qing Dynasty

Yu Tang Fu Gui, the Suzhou Taohuawu New-Year picture, from the Qing Dynasty, printed with wood color woodcut printing techniques.

glossy ganoderma at the front of the book. Their existence proves that color woodcut printing was already used in book printing during that period.

In the late Ming Dynasty (16th–17th century), color woodcut printing became popular. The extant books of this kind are mostly the outputs from families of Min Qiji and Ling Mengchu in Wuxing (today's Zhejiang province) during the Wanli period (1563–1620) of the Ming Dynasty. According to rough statistics, the two families printed 145 kinds of books, 13 kinds of which are three-color prints, four are four-color prints and one is a five-color version. The two families, engaged in the same business for generations, are legends in Chinese printing history.

Color woodcut printing was further developed during the Qing Dynasty. According to *Aggregation of the Carvings in China*, there were more than 40 multi-color block print shops during the Qing Dynasty. The representative overprints at the time are the official versions of the four-color *Guwen Yuanjian*, the two-color *Anthology Selected by Emperors* in the Kangxi period, the four-color *Imperial Tang and Song Collection* as well as the five-color *Chuang-Sian-Jing-Kur* from the Qianlong reign. Private printing also yielded good works such as two popular versions of *Du Gongbu Collection* in the Daoguang Period (1820–1850), one was Lukun's six-color version in Zhuozhou, and the other was Ye Yun'an five-color version in Guangdong.

Common Development and Prosperity—Five Major Publishing Systems

Chinese ancient printing was the most advanced and popular in the world. The foundations of three publishing systems—government, private and bookshop—were settled as early as the Tang and Five Dynasties Period. Besides those three, there were two other quite influential systems: temple and book institutes. Together, they created a unique publishing system. In the long-term development, each system, with distinctive features, contributed to ancient printing and played an immeasurable role in the spread and preservation of ancient books, culture and knowledge.

Annotations of the Book of Rites printed by Fuzhou Gongshiku in 1177

Official printing: government publishing

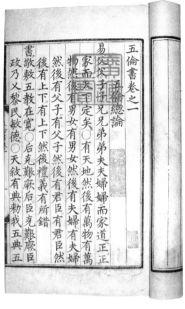

Official printing refers to the publishing sector funded or hosted by the central governmental institutions or local cultural or administrative organizations. Before the invention of printing, governments of many periods were involved in the collection, edition, transcribing and spread of books and records, which never stopped. Due to the low efficiency of transcribing, which was the

Jingchang edition of *Wulunshu* printed during the Zhengtong period of the Ming Dynasty (1436–1450)

main method of reproduction, the scale of publication was also constrained. Not until the invention of printing, did the government's realization of the advantages of printing technology lead to large-scale printing of books. Gradually, an influential official printing system emerged with large capacity and bright characteristics.

Printing by government was started by Feng Dao during the Five Dynasties period. It became prosperous throughout the Song and Yuan dynasties and reached its heyday during the Ming and Qing dynasties. Official printing generally consisted of central and local government printing: the Imperial College in the Song Dynasty, the Central Inner Court in the Ming Dynasty and the Wuyingdian in the Qing Dynasty were the important

Feng Dao and the first printing of Confucian classics
Inspired by popular non-official publishing and to help the public benefit from Confucius classics, Feng Dao (882–954), a prime minister in Later Tang Dynasty and Later Jin Dynasty of Five Dynasties in succession, made a request to the emperor in the third year of Changxing of Later Tang Dynasty (932AD) to have the nine Confucius classics printed based on the Kaicheng Stone Classics. The nine were *I Ching, Book of Odes, The Book of History, Rites of the Zhou, The Book of Rites, Etiquette and Ceremonies, The Zuo Commentary of the Spring and Autumn Annals and The Gongyang Commentary and The Guliang Commentary.* His request was granted and printing commenced in that year but was not concluded until 935. Besides the nine classics, another three books were also printed: *The Annotation of Classics, Classical Characters and Jiujing Ziyang.* Since this project was supervised by the imperial academy, these books are known as the "Jianben version of the nine Confucius classics in the Five Dynasties period." They heralded official book printing in China and had far-reaching impact on the dynasties that followed. For example, the imperial academy during the Song Dynasty used these books as the basis for their reproduction. Feng Dao was also regarded as the founder of major official printing and publishing of Confucian classics in Chinese history.

The inner court copperplate print of *Plowing and Weaving* from the reign of Emperor Kangxi of the Qing Dynasty

institutions of central government printing in their respective times. Gongshiku Printing in the Song Dynasty and Seignior Printing were the representatives of local government printing.

After the Opium War, official printing declined and was gradually replaced by modern publishing. Since its inception, government book printing followed a distinct path, to serve as a tool to influence the public and maintain feudal rule. The content was also quite focused on Confucian classics, historical records and compilations driven by emperors. With strong financial support and talent, the quality of books from this system was guaranteed and served as a model to the whole publishing industry. This sector was also a major contributor to the preservation of ancient classics, the popularization of knowledge and enhancements in the quality of books.

Bookshop printing: non-official publishing

"Shufang" (bookshops), also called *Shulin, Shupu, Shutang* or *Shupeng*, evolved from the *Shusi* of the Han Dynasty. Its predecessors are book stands on the street and book vendors who sold books to pedestrians. After the invention of printing,

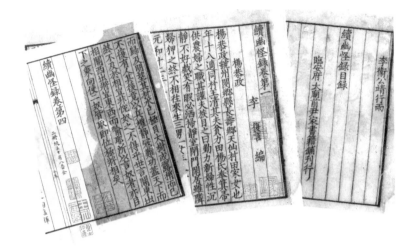

Xuyou Guailu printed by Yin's bookshop of Lin'an in the Song Dynasty

the business scope of bookshops expanded from retail and wholesale to compiling, editing, writing, carving and printing. In essence, it combined the functions of a publishing house, printing workshop and bookstore. Books from this source are oriented to the general public and their ultimate purpose was profit. This type of publishing was more commercial than official and private publishing and is similar to today's private publications.

In the ancient Chinese book printing system, bookshops, with wide distribution, quantity and the greatest impact, were on the upsurge during Tang Dynasty (about the 8th century). They were the major force for the production of ancient books and also the mainstream of commercial book circulation. They adopted block printing first, which laid the foundation for the rise of official and private book printing. Over a thousand years, many famous book printing families emerged, which took great pains to build their businesses, handed down from generation to generation, and enjoyed a lasting significance. Thereby, with a distinctive content and format, they contributed greatly to the spread and preservation of traditional culture. Of the many famous printing families, the most well-known are the Yu's in Jian'an and Chen's in Lin'an during the Song and Yuan dynasties.

Private printing: personal publishing

Private printing refers to privately funded book printing. Most ancient private book printing families were senior officials, rich businessmen or scholars who put a heavy emphasis on the quality of the books. Their books are characterized more by the idea of "working for reputation" and less for their business interest.

Many private book publishers were well-known academics. They combined book printing and studies. In the process of collecting, editing and printing, they also conducted proofreading, critical interpretation, textual research, literate studies and directory compilation and built up and enriched the "Theory of Compiling Books." Some private printers also made bold technical innovations, such as the development of copper type, registration, assembled block printing, blind embossing, and employment of facsimile printing and other techniques to restore and preserve the appearance of ancient editions. Therefore, many of the private printed books are of high quality.

Ancient Chinese private book printing

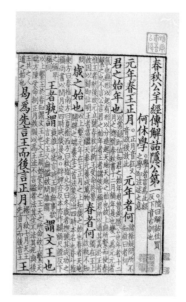

Kung-yang's Commentary on the Spring and Autumn Annals printed by Wanjuantang of Yu Renzhong in 1191

The private edition by Liao Yingzhong of the *Collection of Changli* from the Xianchun period of the Song Dynasty (1265–1274)

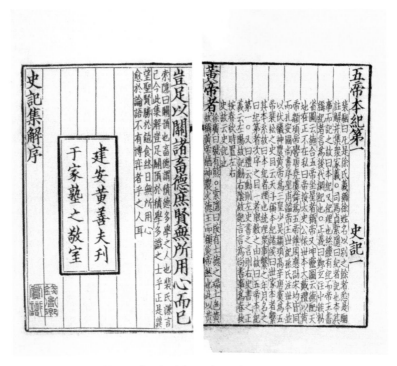

Home school edition of Huang Shanfu of *Annotation to the Record of Grand Historians* in Jian'an of the Song Dynasty

began during the Tang Dynasty. It was popular during the Song Dynasty and shaped the triangular balance with official and bookshop printing, whose output, famous for their high quality, are mostly classic and history works as well as the collections of poems and articles by celebrity.

In the late Ming Dynasty, private printing was more active with the emergence of a group of known private publishers, of which Mao Jin was the most famous during the Ming Dynasty and even through the history of ancient Chinese publishing. Mao Jin (1599–1659) was born in Changshu, Jiangsu Province. He was engaged in private printing from his 30s and built "Jiguge" and "Mugenglou," with a collection of over 80,000 books. Throughout his life, he had high-quality versions of his collection printed.

A picture of Jiguge of Mao Jin in Yushan

With over 600 books and more than 100,000 blocks used, it made him the most productive private publisher in China.

Generally, private printing during the Qing Dynasty fell into two categories. One was writings of past scholars and works by the printer. In most cases, with types based on handwriting as well as selected ink and paper, most of the books from this source were refined products and the editions were also refined. The other category was book series, lost books and old editions printed by book collectors and experts in the restoration of ancient books after the rise of "Theory of Textual Criticism."

College printing: academic publishing

College education represented a unique culture and educational base during the Tang and Song dynasties (618–1279). Originating in the Tang Dynasty, it became popular during the Northern Song and reached its peak in the Southern Song. It continued to the end of Qing Dynasty. According to statistics, there were more than 6,600 colleges throughout the history of

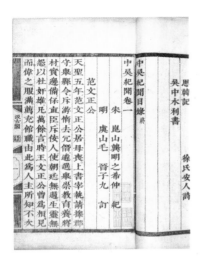

Mao's Jiguge edition of *Zhongwu Jiwen* in the late Ming Dynasty

China. In these colleges, besides lecturing, teaching, writing and academic research, editing and publishing were also regular activities. The result was the formation of the college printing system.

The Song and Yuan dynasties (960–1368) witnessed a boom in college printing. With ample income and capital and also well-known scholars, printing in colleges flourished and produced many good publications. The typical example is *Comprehensive Studies in Administration* by Hangzhou West Lake College in the first year of Taiding (1324). During the Ming and Qing dynasties (1368–1911), publishing by the colleges was further strengthened and large-scale printing became common. The number of books printed by colleges in the Qing Dynasty topped the number from any other period.

The official and private operation of colleges ensured that their publications covered a wide array of topics, including "*Jing*," "*Shi*," "*Zi*" and "*Ji*." At the same time, they were student-centered, so the focus was academic publication, particularly the inheritance from certain schools. College editions can be divided into three types: writing and research notes of teachers and students for academic research, teaching reference works and works by successive masters and famous writings by their principals to spread academic ideas and theories. With an emphasis on academia and abundant funds, college editions are often refined.

Temple and monastery publications: religious publishing

Temple printing refers to publishing of religious classics by temples. These books are called "*Focang*" or "*Daozang*"

Gate of Yuelu College in Changsha City of Hunan Province

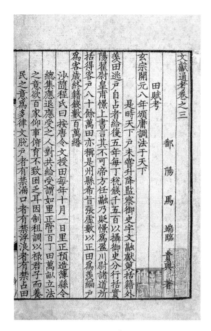

Hangzhou West Lake College printed edition of *Comprehensive Studies in Administration* during the Taiding Period (1324–1328) of Yuan Dynasty

(Taoist canon). They are similar to today's religious publications. Their efforts were supported by governments and Buddhism and Taoist classics were popular. These two factors helped give rise to an independent publishing system.

The most primary outputs of Buddhist temple print shops during the 800 years from the Song to the Qing Dynasty were the 17 Chinese Tripitakas and a number of Tripitakas in minority languages (including Tangut, Mongolian, Tibetan and Manchu). Among all the Tripitikas, *The Northern Song Dynasty Official Version of The Tripitaka* (also known as "*Kaibaozang*") printed in the Kaibao period (968–976) of the Song Dynasty was the first printed Tripitaka in the world.

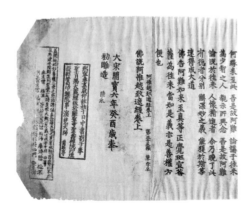

The incomplete page of *Kaibaozang* from Page 4 to 23 printed with government funding in the early Northern Song Dynasty

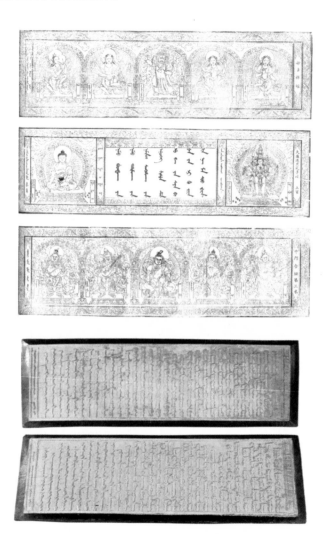

Tripitaka
The so-called *Tripitaka*, equal to a modern large-scale series, are Buddhist canons of scriptures which are a huge collection of all the Buddhist classics organized in a systematic manner. Therein, the first category, the "Vinaya Pitaka," is the code of ethics. The second category, the "Sutra Pitaka" consists primarily of accounts of the Buddha's teachings. The third category is the "Abhidharma Pitaka." *Tripitaka* is also known as "Sanzangjing" or "Yiqiejing." "Zang" in Sanskrit is Pitaka, and it initially referred to a bamboo basket, containing the meaning of the collection. Moreover, *Tripitaka* is always very extensive, usually over 5,000 volumes. With as many as over 100,000 type plates, thousands of people were involved in writing, proofreading, type carving, printing and circulation. It took more than 10 years—and sometimes several decades or a century to complete the work.

The two red-color printed pictures of *Tripitaka* and type plate in Manzhu language, the printing started in 1773 and it took 17 years to complete.

Taoism is a native religion in China. With specific compilation efforts, collections and organizational structure, *Daozang* is a large series of Taoist classics. In addition, the book also contains hundreds of schools of thought and many ancient works of science and technology, including medicine, health, alchemy,

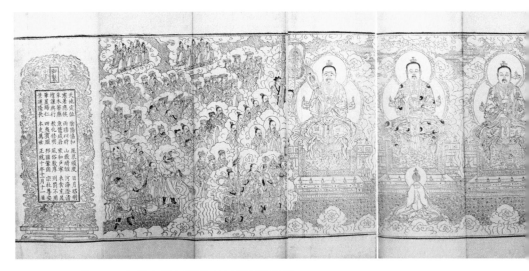

The excerpt of Selection of *Daozang* printed in 1445

astronomy, astrology and other topics.

Compilation of *Daozang* began during the Northern Zhou Dynasty (557–581). During the Zhenghe period of the Song Dynasty (1111–1118), the first printed version of Daozang, *Wanshou Daozang*, whose printing was presided over by the emperor, came out in 5,481 volumes. It was distributed to temples across the nation. With a total of 5,305 volumes, the extant copies of ancient China's *Dacang* are "the orthodox *Daozang*" printed in the Ming Dynasty (1445).

From Bamboo Strips to Stitched Binding: The Ancient Art of Bookbinding and Layout

Taking the invention of papermaking and printing as the demarcation point, the history of books in China can be divided into three phases with a corresponding book system. Bamboo strips and silk manuscripts coexisted before the invention of paper during the Han Dynasty. Scroll roll binding in the paper book period between the Han and Tang dynasties. And the album leaf system popular in the era of printed text after the invention of printing in the Tang Dynasty. Obviously there is some overlapping of these systems.

Jiandu (bamboo and wooden strips)

Before the invention of paper, most Chinese books were written on bamboo or wooden strips. One bamboo strip was called "Jian," and many of them were bound to form a complete document which was known as "Ce." "Jian" and "Ce" were called "Jiance." Processed wooden strips with no characters written on there were called "Ban." Those with characters were called "Du" and thin ones were named "Mujian."

Books made of wooden strips were called "Bandu." For the convenience of reading and collecting books, Many "Jian" were bound with hemp fiber or hide rope and bound "Jian" could be folded with the last piece as the scroll, marking a volume of a book which could be unfolded from the first piece while reading.

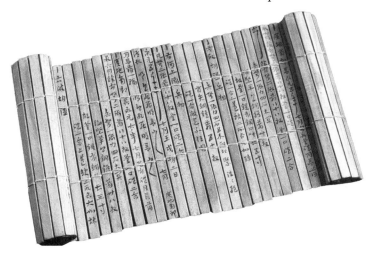

The restoration of Jiandu made of bamboo and wooden strips

This was known as the Jiandu system, which was the earliest form of bookbinding and was used for thousands of years.

In the 5th century, with the wide application of paper and the appearance of paper texts, Jiandu was replaced by paper texts.

The scroll system

The scroll system evolved from the volume system and took its final shape during the time of silk manuscripts. It was further used in the era of paper texts and a complete system was formed that was used to mount books or paintings in modern China.

The procedure was as follows. A piece of wood working as a scroll was stuck on the end of the paper roll, and papers were rolled onto the scroll. Characters written directly onto silk sheets or, in the case of paper texts, pieces of paper with characters were stuck onto the scroll in proper order. A piece of paper or silk

The scroll edition of *Qimin Yaoshu*

with no characters was named "Piao." Solid and resilient, it was attached to the beginning of the books with a scroll roll for the purpose of protection. A string was tied in the top of the "Piao" to bind the scroll. To mark the content of the books and make retrieval easier, a small tablet called "Qian" was often hung on the scroll and some were attached on the end of string, which was fixed after binding.

While reading, the scroll was open and unfolded. After reading, the scroll was rolled, tied by a string and put flat with one end of the scroll facing the outside on a bookshelf. Readers needed to just take them out as needed and insert them back on the shelf later. This system was called "Chajia."

Transition from scroll to album leaf

Accordion binding

Palm sutras in "fanjiazhuang" were introduced from India to China from the 7th to 9th century and gave Chinese scholars inspiration. Rather than folding a long roll, they could be folded back and forth into a rectangular shape. A hard board was used at the front and back to protect the folds into a concertina

A carved copy of *Manchu Tripitaka* in Fanjiazhuang from 1736–1795

Different kinds of concertina bound books collected in the National Palace Museum

binding. These scroll folded into concertina eliminated the need to unroll half a scroll to see a passage in the middle.

Whirlwind binding

Whirlwind binding evolved from scroll rolls. It is shaped like a scroll and based on a long paper on which the first page is stuck. The second page is stuck on the base with a paper scrip from the right side with no characters and other pages are stuck under

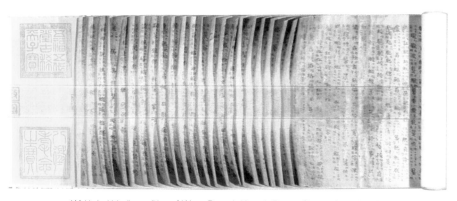

Whirlwind binding edition of *Wang Renxu's Kanmiu Buque Qieyun*, the only existing whirlwind binding example from the Tang Dynasty

the last page from the left side. With pages collected together, the whirlwind binding edition of a book is read from the right side to the left side page after page, and is rolled from the end of the book.

This binding method was called "whirlwind binding" because of the circular movement of the page, which is like a whirlwind. When the book is unfolded, pages are arranged like dragon's scales. Therefore, it is also known as "dragon's scale" binding. *Wang Renxu's Kanmiu Buque Qieyun*, a manuscript from the Tang Dynasty collected in the National Palace Museum is a representative of whirlwind binding.

Album leaf

From the late Tang to the early Song, printed books gradually replaced manuscripts, and album leaf also replaced the scroll system.

Album leaf refers to binding several single leaves into a volume suitable for printing. The earliest album leaf system was butterfly binding, which evolved into wrapped back binding and then stitched binding. When machine based printing was introduced, binding gradually moved to paper and hard-cover binding.

Butterfly binding

The name butterfly binding emerged from its resemblance to a butterfly when the book was spread out. It was the main layout system used during the Song Dynasty. In butterfly binding, two pages were printed on a sheet, which was then folded inwards. The sheets were pasted

Butterfly binding edition of *Dream Pool Essay* from the Yuan Dynasty

together at the fold to make a codex with alternate openings of printed and blank pairs of pages. A hard cover (sometimes coated with cloth or silk) was made. In appearance, it looked like a modern paper or hardcover bound book and the shape of the leaves and the manner in which the book opened and closed resembled the wings of a butterfly.

Wrapped back binding

In wrapped-back binding, pages are folded the opposite way round. Each sheet of paper was only printed on one side but, after folding, the wood block print would appear on the "outside" rather than the "inside" of the folio. These folios were then piled up on top of each other so that the open ends, instead of the

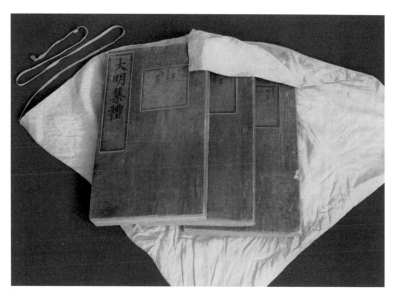

The wrapped back binding version of *Daming Jili*, from the Ming Dynasty

edges, came together to form the spine. Wrapped-back binding appeared during the late Southern Song dynasty and remained in practice after the 16th century. The famous *Yongle Encyclopedia* is an example of a wrapped back edition.

Stitched bound books from the Qing Dynasty

Stitched binding

Stitched binding first appeared in the 16th century. It developed from wrapped back binding. The wood block print would appear on the "outside" rather than the "inside" of the folio. Each group was made up of two or more sheets of paper joined together with thread at the fold. The spines of each of the gatherings are sewn together. The spines of the gatherings are brought together to form the book.

Usually four holes were made on a stitched bound book and such editions were called "four needle eye editions." For larger books, two more holes were punctured. These were called "six needle eye editions." Sometimes thread or silk were used to bind the two corners up and down to protect the books and make them look nice. Such books were called "corner wrapped editions." Another kind of stitched book was called "rough editions" because the pages were not cut to be identical in size after the holes are made. Stitched books are easy to read, durable and practical. This type of binding is still used today for copies of ancient book using deckle edged *paper or rice paper, which gives them a* simple and elegant look.

The appearance of stitch binding represents the last phase in the history of traditional Chinese bookbinding. After the 18th century, machine based printing gradually adopted the appearance of paperback and hard cover books.

Layout of printed edition

All woodblock printed books are printed on one side of the page only and each page has a certain format. Usually a single page format includes layout, boundary box, boundary line, core, fish tail, trunk, head, foot, ear and so on.

Typeface: The area of one type.

Type frame: Black lines around a typeface are also called boundary lines. A single line frame is called a single boundary line while a double line frame was called double line boundary.

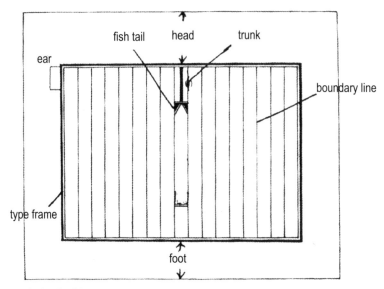

Ancient book layout

Manuscripts of *History of Qing Court*, red silk line version from 1736–1795

The boundary was usually thicker outside and thinner inside.

Boundary line: Lines to mark outlines, lines painted with black, red and blue ink are called "black thread line," "red thread line" and "blue thread line," named thanks to the thin boundary line.

Head and foot: The upper part outside a typeface is the head. The bottom is the foot.

Heart: A narrow line in the centre of the typeface.

Fish tail: A graphic resembling a fish tail at about a quarter of the way to the centre of the heart. The fish tail divides the heart into three parts. The centre is for the title, number of volume and page number. The upper part for the page number and later book title, sometimes the publisher's name also appears here. The lower part for the type carver's name and, later, the publisher's name or name of the book series.

Trunk: The part between the fish tail and the frame. The trunk printed with black lines was called "heikou." It is called "xi heikou" if the line is thin and "cu heikou" if it is thick. In the absence of line or character, it is called "baikou."

Ear: Small box at the upper part of the boundary lines, usually for the name of the passage.

Structure of printed edition

The appearance of an ancient book includes the book clothes, book mark, protection page, cover page, book spine, book mouth, book brain, book head, book root and wrapped corner, and so on.

Book clothes: Now called the cover, usually made using colored hard paper to protect the book, hence the name.

Book mark: Paper mark used to write the book title and pasted on the book clothes, usually inscribed by celebrities or teachers.

Protection page: Also called title page, it is a blank page inside the book.

Cover page: Cover in ancient times referred to the first page after the protection page. The title was written on it, usually by someone famous.

Wrapped corner of the stitched bound *Shiqu Baoji* manuscript from 1736–1795

Book spine: One end of the binding, also called book back.

Book mouth: The opposite side of the spine.

Book brain: Places where holes are punched for thread to go through. In modern hard-cover editions, the places where staples go into are also called the book brain,

Book head: Refers to the cut on the top.

Book root: Refers to the cut at the bottom.

Wrapped corner: Corners wrapped with silk, to protect the book and also make it look neat.

The Course of Inheritance
Collection, Preservation and Spread of Chinese Books

Over the thousands of years' history of the publishing industry in ancient China, the number and variety of books continued to grow alongside the development of society and culture. At the same time, man-made destruction (bans, war, theft, etc.) and natural disasters (water, fire, insects, etc.), and other factors led to the loss and disappearance of books. Such loss is very serious. A number of major book disasters caused immeasurable loss to ancient Chinese culture. To address this issue, ancient Chinese invented various ways to preserve books. Their efforts gave rise to the colorful and time-honored history of collection, which included taking good care of books, building more collection houses and taking measures to protect books. The history of collection, taking the "Cangshi" for management of oracle records during the Shang and Zhou dynasties as its inception to the emergence of modern libraries in the early twentieth century, is over 3,000 years old. It has a

Jiayetang Library in Huzhou, Zhejiang, completed in 1924, which is strongly reminiscent of a traditional collection house.

unique position in the history of book collecting in the world.

In general, the book-collecting house in ancient China considered with respect to book reservation rather than circulation, which made a certain distinction between book-collecting house and library in modern times. The publishing industry in ancient China, mainly circulating through sale in book market, transcription and borrow, interiorly formed the book trade and circulating system with non-official book market base, exteriorly shaped the famed book road in the exchange of publishing industries home and abroad, actively facilitated the cultural exchanges.

Bibliophiles and Book-collecting House

Book collection in ancient China can be divided into four categories: Official collection, private collection, temple collection and college collection. As a main channel for the protection of ancient books and records, the first two achieved greater success. Traditional book collectors are private while "Changshulou," or book collection house, are structures used for book preservation, including those ran by official organizations, private groups or individuals. In ancient China, the mainstay for book collection, management, research, proofreading and publication is official and non-official libraries. These buildings, together with collectors linked to them, preserved and spread a wealth of ancient books and records and the extensive and profound history and culture of China.

Book collection in ancient China started during the Xia and Shang dynasties. Unearthed oracle bones from Anyang in Henan Province show that Shang period historiographers and wizards were already aware of the importance of preserving and colleting documents and literature. The collection of oracle bones was the earliest form of book collecting.

Formal book collection started at the Zhou Dynasty. The book-collecting institutions in the period respectively bored the varies names such as "Tianfu," "Mengfu," "Cefu," "Zhoufu," "Storehouse" and "Privy Chambers"; the various positions, divided into "Mahavamsa," "Xiaoshi," "Neishi," "Waishi," "Zuoshi" and "Youshi," for the historiographer in charge, which reflected the scale and divisions of the official

Image of Laozi, who was once an official in the Zhou Dynasty's state collection agency, and is known as the earliest curator of China's national library.

collection institutions in the Zhou Dynasty. Reportedly the famous thinker Laozi once worked as a historiographer of the Zhou Dynasty's "Cangshi," an equivalent to a curator of a national library nowadays. There are several known private book collectors from that time including the famous scholar Hui Shi (370–310B.C.) who had five carriages of books, a huge collection at the time.

Despite the first emperor Qinshihuang's order to burn and destroy books after the unification of the country, official book collecting never stopped. During his reign, several book collection organizations were set up in the Erpang Palace in Xianyang such as Mingtang and Shishi. Specific officials were designated to manage them. Resistance to the imperial order of destroy books was widespread as various ways were invented

Shiqu Baoji, inner court manuscript, the title still indicates influence from Han Dynasty's collection houses.

to preserve books. It was against this background that the story of keeping books in Eryou unfolds. According to the story, at the end of Qin Dynasty, to avoid damage from wars, a scholar moved all his books to caves in Dayou and Eryou Hills in Hunan Province. Generations later they were found. These books were called the "collection from the Eryou stone chambers." A Ming scholar, Hu Yinglin (1551–1602), touched by ancestral passion for books and study, named his book collection room "Eryou Shanfang."

In the early days of the Western Han period, the minister Xiao He (?–193 B.C.) presided over the construction of three imperial libraries, called Shiquge, Tianluge and Qilinge, to collect books and archives. Later, Shiqu and Tianlu became another name for imperial collections. As an attempt to protect books from fire and water, libraries in the Han Dynasty were made of stone and called "Shishi" or stone chambers. While the bookcases were coated with copper sheet and called "Jinkui" or golden casket. Afterwards, these two names became terms for the structures used to house imperial books collections. A group of famous book collectors also emerged during the Han Dynasty.

After the founding of the Eastern Han Dynasty, book

The Tianyige outlook, the earliest existing private collection house in China

collection resumed and books were kept in Dongguan, Lantai and some other locations. When in peak collection, there were enough books to fill over 6,000 carts. Of the seven libraries in this period, the most famous ones are Lantai and Dongguan, which played a role in proofreading, editing and writing besides their part in collecting books. In 159A.D, the first organization in the feudal central government, in charge of book collection and proofreading, was set up. The archival bureau, as it was called, functioned for 1,500 years.

Despite books could not expect to be immune from the results of constant turmoil and wars during the Three Kingdoms, the Jin Dynasty, Northern and Southern Dynasties, it was gradually borne in on the rulers that the significance and value of collecting books. Once wars finished, book collection would resume. By then, the main collector was still the archival bureau. During the Sui Dynasty, two emperors once ordered the extensive collection had 50 copies for each sort and the copies were sheltered in the Guanwendian in the capital of Luoyang. Another location with a high concentration of books was Chang'an, where 370,000 rolls of books were deposited in Jiazedian.

By the Tang Dynasty, management of books was quite developed and libraries also took up functions of editing and proofreading. Most books were collected in the archival bureau and managed by the director of the archival bureau. In addition, there were Hongwenguan, Shiguan, Jixianguan (collectively called Sanguan) as well as Chongwenyuan, Sijingyuan and Hanlinyuan, which were independent but closely related to each other. For example, the major function of Hongwenguan was to collect and proofread books; Shiguan was responsible for book writing and collection set up in the Zhenguan period; Jixianyuan was the largest state library in the middle term of the Tang Dynasty and also the most complete with a collection exceeding any other. Chongwenyuan was a school set up for princes in the Zhenguan period, but also functioned in terms of book collection, proofreading and transcription; Sijingju, specially providing service for princes, was an organization in charge of book affairs in the East Palace; Hanlinyuan was a consulting organization to draft emperor's

Huangshicheng and jinkui inside the deposited archives

Outlook of the Iron Qin Bronze Sword Tower of the Qu's in Changshu, Jiangsu.

ordinances, so book collection was meant to assist this function. This system of collection had far-reaching influence on following generations. During this dynasty, the number of private collectors was larger than the sum of previous generations.

The spread of woodblock printing promoted the development of official and private book collections during the Song and Yuan dynasties. During the Song, the national collection agencies were Shiguan, Zhaowenguan and Jixianyuan and later Chongwenguan which was built on the collection efforts from the three earlier agencies. In addition, there were other agencies like Mige, Taiqinglou and Liuge. Among them, Mige housed some 10,000 volumes selected from the three agencies, which represent the essence of the national library. College and private collections were well developed during the Song Dynasty, the well-known bibliophiles, as Ye Mengde (1077–1148), Chao Gongwu (1105–1180), Zheng Qiao (1104–1162), Chen Zhensun (about 1183–1262) and others, each

Outlook of Guyue Library in Shaoxing, Zhejiang, the first public library in the modern history of China.

had collections with more than 10,000 volumes. In addition, the preparation of private collection directories also witnessed a series of breakthroughs, which made private collections more academic. During the Yuan Dynasty, the archival bureau was set in charge of book affairs and the specialized agencies in charge of printing under the supervision of the archival bureau. State collection during the Yuan Dynasty inherited features from the Southern Song, putting equal emphasis on both manuscripts and printed versions.

Academic and cultural prosperity during the Ming Dynasty combined with more developments in printing helped official and private collections prosper beyond those of previous generations. During the Ming Dynasty, the national collection agency was Wenyuange. The independent specialized state agency of book supervision was the archival bureau, later replaced by the Hanlinyuan. In addition, in 1534, the Ming Dynasty built an archive warehouse for imperial files and works called Huangshicheng. This was the most complete existing imperial library complex. During this period, private collection was very popular and the size of libraries was also expanded. Most collectors were to be found in the economic and cultural prosperous south-east. One of the most prestigious private libraries was the Tianyi Pavilion of the Fans in Ningbo, Jiguge of the Mao's in Changshu and Danshengtang of the Qi's in Shanyin. Built in 1561, during the Ming Dynasty, Tianyige housed 70,000 volumes and survives to this day. It is the earliest private library still in existence in China.

Most state collections during the Qing Dynasty were housed in the inner court, in Huangshicheng, Zhaorendian, Wuyingdian, Chizaotang, Yangxindian, Nanxundian, Ziguangge and Nanshufang. The seven copies of *Siku Quanshu* compiled during Qianlong's reign were deposited in seven different places. The three in the south were open to learners, which made them function like public libraries.

Of the 1,175 collectors recorded by scholar Ye ChangChi (1849–1931) in his Poems about Collecting Books, 497 were from the Qing Dynasty. During the middle of the Qing Dynasty, four famous libraries emerged: Haiyuange by Yang Yizeng in Liaocheng, Iron Qin Bronze Sword Tower by Qu Shaoji in Changshu, Bisonglou by Lu Xinyuan in Gui'an and 8,000-Roll Tower by Ding Shen and Ding Bing in Hangzhou. The four libraries possessed many precious books from the Song and Yuan dynasties. Even after the damage from wars and fire, Haiyuange still had over 219,000 volumes.

In the early twentieth century, with the introduction of modern libraries from the west, the traditional Chinese libraries gradually went downhill. Some opened their doors to the public, transforming themselves into modern libraries and ending the ancient Chinese tradition of private library undertakings.

Effective Ways to Protect Books

Over the long history of imperial and private book collection, special attention was given to the protection of books. Therefore, a complete set of techniques and methods were developed, which are still useful today. Generally in order to address theft, tainting and other human damage, the following two approaches would be involved:

The first was classified arrangement and management. Some books were arranged according to content. For example, in Guanwendian, during the Sui Dynasty, Confucian classics and history books were kept in the east chamber; philosophy and literature books in the west chamber. Tang Dynasty book collector Li Bi used red toothpicks to mark Confucian classics books, green for the history, blue for the philosophy and white for the literature. The practice was similar to modern category management and is very practical. Some arranged books

A corner of the rare book section in Shouan Palace of the Forbidden City, preservation still follows many practices in ancient collection houses.

Baoshulou, one scene in Tianyige

according to quality. For example, book collection agencies in the Sui Dynasty used red colored glaze scrolls for the best quality books, black and red for ordinary books and black for sub-standard books. Similarly, in modern libraries, books are also classified as rare and ordinary editions. Some managed books based on their function. For example, Liu Gongchuo (763–830) from the Tang Dynasty had over 10,000 volumes and each one had three different versions, the best one deposited, a medium quality one for daily reading and lesser quality ones for beginners to learn. Such classification may well be termed unique insight to facilitate use and protection of books.

The second was strict restrictions on readers. Encouraged by the value of their possessions, private and official libraries were generally closed to the public, making them quite inaccessible. For example, the imperial collection was not supposed to be read by ordinary people; even senior officials had to follow very strict rules. Private collectors adopted a similar practice. For example, during the Ming Dynasty, Fan Qin (1506–1585)

made it an explicit family rule that the books in Tianyige were not for lending and not to be taken outside the building. He had each and every one of his sons hold one key to the book house. Only when every son was present could the lock be opened. Books were not lent to outsiders; anyone within the family who wanted to read could do that inside the house during daytime. Smoking was strictly prohibited. Some other collectors allowed lending or outsiders in their library but with very stringent rules attached. For example, the book collector Ye Dehui (1864–1927) made it clear that whoever could not go inside his library without his company. No servants were allowed to follow. Winter coats or loose clothing were not allowed inside the library. Long conversations had to be held outside.

These rules may have their limitation but still served as some kind of protection to the books and avoided losses and theft.

Natural hazards to books are fire, water and insects. Against these problems the ancient preservation techniques of books was also soundly developed. The main methods were the following four:

Architectural protection

The artistic values and practical functions were ingeniously integrated in the buildings of many ancient libraries, which embodiedthe the great wisdom and profound cultural connotations. For example, "Shishi" and "Jinkui" in the Han Dynasty were designed as a measure against fire. In terms of architectural protection, the design and construct of Tianyige in the Ming Dynasty was also advanced at the time. Tianyige has two stories, the one above is a complete hall; the other below is separated into six chambers to prevent moisture damage. All the books are deposited on the second floor with windows at the front and back. Shelves were spaced out and doors were placed in front and behind the book cabinets for ventilation. Insecticidal herbs were also placed in cabinets. To prevent fires, a pond was dug in front of the library, which is called Tianyi Pond. Only in this way, could much damage caused by natural hazards be efficiently reduced.

Dyed paper

Even in the days of bamboo and wood strips, the treatment of drying green bamboo strips on the fire "Shaqing"—was used to extend the life of bamboo strips. After the invention of paper, dying was used in order to prevent the paper from insects and worms.

As early as the Han and Wei periods, people used juice from boiled Huangbo or cork to stain paper and protect it from insects. This dyeing process is called "Ruhuang" and it gives the paper slightly yellow tint. For example, most of the sutras preserved in the Dunhuang Grottoes from the Tang Dynasty were stained yellow. Despite some broken parts, the paper is in good condition without any worm damage after over 1,000 years.

During the Song Dynasty, a new method was invented. Paper was soaked in Sichuan pepper solution. The chemical composition and strong pungent odor of the pepper have a repellent effect on worms. During the Ming and Qing dynasties, in order to prevent the multitudes of bookworms caused by humid weather in the south, a special paper called "10,000-year red paper" or wannian hongzhi was invented. This type of paper was prepared by painting paper with lead oxide. It was often used in sealed papers or as backing. The white and red combination looks neat and also prevents worm damage.

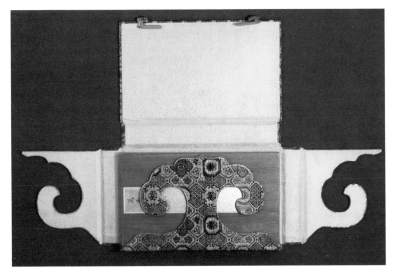

Slipcase with ruyi and cloud pattern in the refined manuscript "*Eighty-Year Birthday Celebration*" from the Qing Dynasty

Chemical approaches

Pest control agents or insecticides were purposely placed in stack room to prevent books from damage by bookworms. Ancient people also had good recipes for it. "*Qimin Yaoshu*" mentioned that musk and papaya could be place on bookshelves to prevent worms. Later herb-of-grace was put in libraries to prevent insects. It is very effective and it is practiced today in some libraries. Besides, the ancients also placed realgar and lime under bookcases, tobacco and cinnamon inside them to prevent book worms.

Layout protection

A spill of rolled paper, besides thread, was used in book binding so that the books were still undispersed even when threads broke. Sandalwood and nanmu were also used to make book sheaths. In order to implement insect prevention and save wear and tear, high quality silky cloth was employed to package books.

In addition, people would also air books on the sunny and dry days in early spring or mid autumn, which could help rid the books of moisture and insects. The aired books, when completely cooled down, were put back into cabinets afterwards. There were also many factors to consider in regards to timing and ways of airing.

The Circulation of the Ancient Books

There was an early record about the circulation of books in ancient China. The rising of civil bookstore marked the formal start of book trade in ancient China. After the spread of printing technique, the quickening velocity and enlarging scope in book trade shaped a huge book-distributing network system and numerous book trade centers.

Extravagant gold plated bookcase for "homage to the bodhisattva Manjusri"

Pushuting or book airing pavilion owned by Zhu Yizun, a private collector from the Qing Dynasty in Jiaxing, Zhejiang

Bookstore and "Huaishi"

Not later than the later period of the 1st century B.C, the earliest civil bookstore in Chinese history emerged in the capital Chang'an and some economically and culturally developed cities.

The bookstores run by civil merchant, with profit purpose, various books, flexible operation, open-selling and free-reading, not only attracted readers, but also well meet the self-study need of the poor intellectuals. Objectively, they played the part of public library which was inexistent at the time, and was well received by readers. The historical documents have many reading-buying books stories about celebrities. There is one that goes: The famous scholar Wang Chong (27–about 97 A.D.) could not afford books because of his poor family background and was a frequent reader in bookstore.

The emergence of numerous bookstores, facilitating book circulation and utility, was also an important means to supplement the official and individual book collections. In the progressive process, the business of bookstore was booming, with the operating procedure of mobile and home book service, and manifested an enriched flavor of commerciality. Stimulated by commercial profit, book peddlers at the time carried about books to the gathering places of Confucian scholars, which gradually led to the being of book market.

From the end of the Western Han Dynasty (1–8 A.D.) to the Xin Dynasty (9–23 A.D.), the earliest book market, "Huaishi," in ancient China turned up near the Imperial College in Chang'an city. At the end of the Western Han Dynasty, Wang Mang was in power that ordered to enlarge the Imperial College, increased the number of the college student and assigned numerous scholars to hold a post in the capital. The gathering of scholars and students promoted the demand of books. Upon that, a comprehensive market including book trade shaped near the Imperial College. The market was called "Huaishi" for the several hundreds of locust trees there.

Different from civil bookstore, the "Huaishi" bore the following distinctive features. First was regularity. The market held semimonthly; second, the main entry party was college student in Chang'an; third, the buying and selling of goods included musical instrument, locally grown products and etc except for books; the fourth was the function of communication and learning exchanges. The academic discussions were frequently held when in the purchase of books; the last was that "Huaishi" was under the official influence and supervision, a specialized institution set by the government monitored the "Huaishi." As a business transaction center, the "Huaishi" possesses an enriched cultural flavour. In 23 A.D., Wang Mang's regime collapsed. With the Imperial College dissolved, the "Huaishi" vanished. Although it survived only over 20 years, the "Huaishi" still exerted a great far-reaching influence on history. The "Huaishi" was often chanted as cultural icons in poems by poets and scholars of later generations.

Book duplicator: "Yongshu"

Before the invention of engraving printing technique, all the books were manual copied, the process was both a continuation of book production and a manifestation mode of book circulation. In Han dynasty there were persons taking book copying as occupation, who were call "Yongshu" in history. The government at the time, set a special post for book copying, employed a great many of "Yongshu" to copy books.

The "Yongshu" at the time, with a comfortable salary, could at least manage to support the family. During the copying process, the "Yongshu" read a lot and accumulate knowledge for fame and officialdom. Look through history record, such big-timers among the numerous "Yongshu" are by no means rare. The famous general Ban Chao (32–102 A.D.), one of

"Proofreading Scene," drawn in the Northern Qi Dynasty (550–577) (this is the tracing image in the Song Dynasty), mirroring the state of book copying and proofreading at the time.

numerous "Yongshu" in the Eastern Han Dynasty, was poor when he was young. Therefore, he had to frequently go to the government organizations for book copying to support his aged mother. Once when copying books, he suddenly cast away his writing brush, sighing, a great man should fight on the battlefield to build his fame and officialdom, how could he wrong himself to undertake the long-term book copying? With his great effort, Ban Chao really became a famous general. This is the noted allusion "Giving up civilian pursuits to join the army" in Chinese history.

The book copying by numerous "Yongshu," promoting book reproduction at the time, contributed significantly to the spread of cultural knowledge. Not for self-study but on the purpose of making living, it is a publishing phenomenon of manual duplicating work, which makes no essential distinction from the subsequent publishers.

Bookstore with printing works in the printing age

During the printing age, book distribution and circulation in China enjoyed a tremendous growth. Thanks to the spread of printing technique, the printing books, with lavish varieties, various norms, huge quantity and excellent quality, swarmed into society and became main selling-books in book market. Drawn by the sound profit, More civil and official people or agencies devoted into book production and trade,which further facilitated the booming of book trade.

In the printing age, Bookstore with printing works run by the civil booksellers played the main part in book trade. As a multi-role of editorial office, printing works and bookstore, bookstore with printing works, seeking profit, printing books as commodity and selling books in market, bored three terms of missions including engraving, printing and selling business. Its primary mission and purpose were rapidly selling books

The present-look of Liulichang in Beijing, once a famed national book trading market in Qing Dynasty and the Republic of China.

in large quantities. With the emergence of more bookstores with printing works, came the competition in the business. Therefore, business promotion was high on the owners' agenda in businesses of every variety: As to the better-selling book, one after another following suit; Therewith, numerous versions of the same book appearing in the same market at the nearly same time; a great increase in advertisement helping to obtain advantage; In addition, some booksellers travelling about with selling-books, some even doing book trade in minority areas or abroad, all these, to a certain extent, promoted the extensive spread of Chinese books and culture.

At that time, not only the civil professional booksellers but also many scholars, government officials and average people involved into book trade in succession. The Confucian philosopher, Zhu Xi in the Song Dynasty (1130–1200) once printed Confucian classics and wrote books for selling, who, with high quality, varieties of books, frequently enjoyed the doorstep selling.

The prosperity of book trade helped to shape the national book market: Therewith, Xiangguo Temple in Kaifeng city in the Northern Song Dynasty, Three Hills Street in Nanjing city in Ming Dynasty and Liulichang in Beijing city in Qing Dynasty, with a tremendous, prosperous book market, became a famed national book trading center in China at the time.

Crystallization of Chinese Culture
Distinctive Chinese Publications

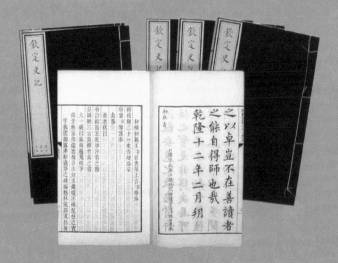

Ancient Chinese books, the most significant and direct output of ancient Chinese publishing, are good indicators of the tremendous number of publications handwritten or printed before 1911. With a long history and strength in numbers, by a conservative estimate there were no less than 100,000 different ancient books. Ancient Chinese books, embodying a concentrated reflection of the splendor of Chinese history and culture, are not only a flourishing symbol of the Chinese publishing industry, but also a crystallization of ancient Chinese wisdom and traditional culture.

From the 7th century onwards, ancient Chinese books were classified into four categories: *"Jing, Shi, Zi and Ji."* "The Thirteen Confucian Classics" are part of *"Jing,"* the "Twenty-five Histories" are *"Shi,"* the "Selected Readings of Confucian and other Ancient Chinese Classics" are *"Zi"* and the "Poems and Prose Works" are *"Ji,"* together they offera more concentrated reflection of the characteristics of Chinese culture. In addition, numerous large reference books and series books bore another feature of broad Chinese culture. Among them, the *Yongle Encyclopedia* and *The Compendium of Works of the Past and the Present* are reference books and the *Siku Quanshu* are series books, both typical representatives of the brilliant achievements of China's ancient publishing industry.

The publishing industry in contemporary China continues the fine tradition of the ancient publishing industry. It publishes and republishes more than 100,000 different books every year. Among them there is no lack of outstanding publications that represent the level of publishing and cultural achievement of Contemporary China such as *Revised Continuation of Siku Quanshu, Zhonghua Dazang Jing* (an encyclopedia of Tibetan studies in 150 volumes), *Encyclopedia of China,* etc.

The Thirteen Confucian Classics

In the 2,000-plus years of feudal society, Confucian culture occupied a leading place in China. Confucian works were so decidedly superior to others that the works about the study and interpretation of Confucian classics came out one after another in massive numbers, shaping the unique study of "Confucian classics."

"Confucian Classics" are books compiled by the Confucians with Confucius as their representative and generally endorsed by Chinese feudal governments. The study of the academic

system was formed by the remarks and themes of the feudal governments, intellectuals and bureaucrats throughout the dynasties. As a result, there is a peculiar phenomenon in Chinese cultural history and Chinese book history, which is the belief that the "study of Confucian classics is superior, other learning is inferior; the study of Confucian classics is the main theme and other studies are sub-themes."

In ancient China, 13 works called the *Thirteen Confucian Classics*, were regarded as the most important. They were *I Ching, Shangshu, the Book of Odes, the Chou Rituals, the Book Ceremony and Ritual, the Book of Rites, the Zuo's Commentary of the Spring and Autumn Annals, the Gongyang Commentary of the Spring and Autumn Annals, the Guliang Commentary of the Spring and Autumn*

The rubbing of "Confucius teaching." Confucius was the founder of Confucianism and is closely associated with Confucian Classics.

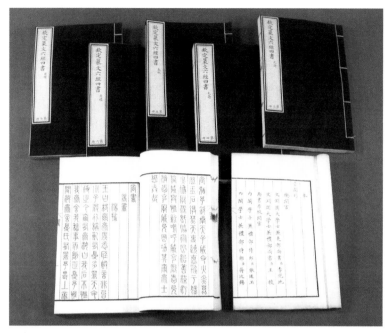

A carving copy of the *Seal Characters of the Six Confucian Classics and the Four Books*, from the reign of Emperor Kangxi of the Qing Dynasty.
The *Four Books* refers to the books comprising *The Great Learning*, *The Doctrine of the Mean*, *The Analects of Confucius* and *Mencius*.

Annals, the *Analects of Confucius,* the *Book of Filial Piety, Erya,* and *Mencius.*

As Confucian classics, no other old works can parallel the Thirteen Confucian Classics in terms of position as well as a deep and broad influence. With them as the focus, a large number of derivative works about the Study of Confucian classics emerged. Those works are hundreds of times more numbers than the Thirteen Confucian Classics, which total 650,000 words. There are more than 4,000 books with 50,000 volumes dedicated to interpreting the classics. These interpretations have become one of the most important and richest types of ancient Chinese books.

With a wide range of knowledge, the Thirteen Confucian Classics, as the basic works of Confucian culture, are the

The majestic carved copy of the *Annotation of the Classics of the Spring and Autumn Period* in the Shu Area (now Sichuan Province) during the Song Dynasty

significant works of Chinese traditional academy. The *I Ching,* the highest in rank, is given first priority over the Thirteen Confucian classics. Originally a book of divination, it is based on the "Yin, Yang and Eight Diagrams," which is externally mysterious but profoundly imbedded with philosophy.

Shangshu documents ancient times. Its main component is royal proclamations and minutes of talks between the emperor and his subjects. It shows the impact of the Five Elements (gold, wood, water, fire and earth) having a significant impact on Chinese thinking.

The Book of Odes, dating from the early Western Zhou Dynasty to the middle of the Spring and Autumn Period and contains the earliest poetic syllogism in China. It is regarded as the model for tradition Chinese poems, which include The Ballads, The Dynastic Hymns, and The Sacrificial Songs. The Ballads refers to the chants of the vassal states during the Zhou Dynasty; the Dynastic Hymns includes court music and part of the rites and music in the territory controlled Zhou Dynasty; the Sacrificial Songs described sacred dance music and poems for the upper classes in the ancestral temple.

The Chou Rituals, The Book of Ceremony and Ritual and *The Book of Rites*, which settles the moral principles in Chinese traditional society, are called the *"Three Etiquettes." The Chou Rituals* collects the bureaucratic establishments in Zhou Dynasty and various states' systems in the Warring States Period; *The Book Ceremony and Ritual* records the etiquette system of the Spring and Autumn

The inner-court carved copy of *The Original Meaning of I Ching* during Emperor Kangxi's reign during the Qing Dynasty. The *I Ching* was given priority to the Thirteen Confucian Classics. To this day there are numerous works on it.

and the Warring States Periods; *The Book of Rites* compiles the works about various etiquettes before the Qin and Han dynasties.

The *Zuo's Commentary of the Spring and Autumn Annals*, *The Gongyang Commentary of the Spring and Autumn Annals* and *The Guliang Commentary of the Spring and Autumn Annals*, which are formed around "The Spring and Autumn Annals," are called the "Three Records of the Spring and Autumn Annals." *The Spring and Autumn Annals* is the history book of annalistic style based on the book of the Lu State by Confucius.

The *Zuo's Commentary of the Spring and Autumn Annals* focuses on the historical events in *The Spring and Autumn Annals*. It also aims to elucidate the arguments in T*he Spring and Autumn Annals*. *The Analects of Confucius*, the most widely read Confucian classic in ancient China, is the records of the words and deeds of

Confucius and his disciples which is the most magisterial account of Confucianism.

The Book of Filial Piety, is based on the idea of ruling the world with filial piety. It discusses feudal filial duty. It is the only Confucian classic in *The Thirteen Classics, Annotated and Explicated* annotated by Emperor Xuanzong of the Tang Dynasty. *Erya*, an interpretation book that explains word meanings and annotates names and descriptions, is the only ancient lexicon regarded as a classic in ancient China for scholars of Confucian classics.

Mencius is devoted to Mencius' words, thought and deeds, whose central idea is promoting a policy of benevolence.

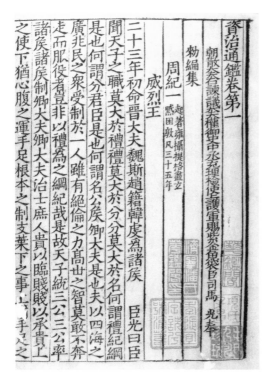

The Gongshiku edition of the *Comprehensive Mirror for the Aid of Government*, the masterpiece of Chinese chronicles from the Song Dynasty during the reign of Emperor Gaozong.

The History of the Twenty-five Dynasties

Worship of the past and an emphasis on history is a notable feature of Chinese culture. Generations of rulers in China attached great importance to the continuity and succession of ancient history and had a tradition of recording the history of the previous dynasty. The system ensured the consistence and continuity of history books. Privately written history books were also very popular. History books rank below *Jing* but far exceed them in terms of total number, type,

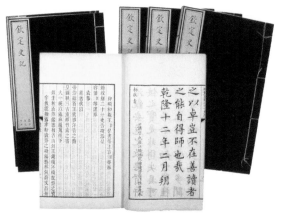

The Records of the Grand Historian, one of 24 historical books printed during the reign of Emperor Qianlong of the Qing Dynasty

variety and style.

History books from ancient China come mainly in three types: Character-centered biographies, chronological records of history and event-centered chronicles. Among them, *The Records of the Grand Historian* is regarded as an official edition. Emperor Qianlong designated it and other histories of 23 dynasties, including the *History of the Ming Dynasty* completed in 1739 as the Histories of Twenty-four Dynasties, making them official. The completion of the *Draft History of the Qing Dynasty* in 1927 added the 25th to this collection. Together, they include 3,795 volumes, recording non-stop history from the legendary Yellow Emperor to 1911 and making it an unparalleled encyclopedia of Chinese history.

The History of Twenty-five Dynasties is presented as a series of biographies that chronicle historical events. In terms of style, the history book presented in a series of biographies can be divided into *"Benji," "Shijia," "Liezhuan," "Shuzhi"* and *"Shibiao."*

Benji refers to the chronological record of

The Earliest Biographical Work of Ancient History in China: *The Records of the Grand Historian*

The Records of the Grand Historian, the earliest biographical work of ancient history in China, written by Sima Qian (145–90B. C.), a famous Western Han historian, is also the finest historical book in China. Leading the "Twenty-four Histories," *The Records of the Grand Historian*, also called *Tai Shi Gong Shu*, covering a history of 3,000 years ranging from the legendary Huang Di, or Yellow Emperor, to the first year of Yuanshou Period of Emperor Wudi of the Han Dynasty (122 B.C.) consists of 130 pieces with 520 thousand words.

With the biographical historiography originated in the book followed by the later official history and a far-reaching influence on the later development of history and literature, *The Records of the Grand Historian*, as an excellent work of literature, occupies an important position in Chinese literary history.

imperial deeds; *Shijia* to histories of noted families; *Liezhuan* to biographies; *Shuzhi* to other histories of diverse institutions, systems, nature, society and etc; and *Shibiao* to a historical lists of intricate social circumstances and figures that are not included in other biographies. These four sections interact and combine to form the whole of a history book.

Yongle Encyclopedia

Leishu or reference books are also special. These books collect all the materials related to a certain category and compile them by category or rhythm to facilitate searching and citing. Because of the wide coverage and rich information these were known as the encyclopedias of ancient times. The first reference book, *The Imperial Reader*, was compiled in 220 A.D. It included more than 40 categories with more than eight million words. By the end of the 19th century, over 700 reference books had been put together. The largest was the *Yongle Encyclopedia* and the most complete was *The Compendium of Works of the Past and the Present*.

The *Yongle Encyclopedia* was commissioned in 1403 (the 6th year of the reign of Emperor Chengzu of the Ming Dynasty, whose imperial title was Yongle) and completed five years later. All together, 2,169 people were involved in the compilation. More than 1,300 were involved just in the transcription. It is one of the best-known manuscripts from the heyday of block printing. It includes 22,937 manuscript rolls, 11,095 volumes and about 370 million Chinese characters, making it an encyclopedia in the real sense. Besides the impressive scale, all the characters were written in neat brush standard script decorated with many dedicate illustrations, red periods and commas. The book sheet size was big, covered with graceful yellow hard back and in wrapped back binding.

Unlike previous reference books, the *Yongle Encyclopedia* used

Binding of the *Yongle Encyclopedia*

A partial copy of extant *Yongle Encyclopedia*

The entry for "门" in the *Yongle Encyclopedia*

rhyme to organize the first words, which hugely facilitated retrieval. Based on the rhyme groups set out in *The Rhymes Dictionary of Hongwu*, the official rhymes dictionary compiled in the beginning of the Ming Dynasty, all characters in different rhyme groups were arranged in the *Yongle Encyclopedia*. Detailed explanations about the meanings of each character was given, followed by different ways of writing characters and parts summaries, allusions, poems, essays and so on. All the information about the characters were collected and listed and all quotations were from the original classics.

Quotations were written with a writing brush dipped in red ink and other information with black ink. With a clear structure and columns and compiled in a way similar to the method used to this day, the *Yongle Encyclopedia* is regarded as the world's first and biggest encyclopedia.

The number of citations and scope of the *Yongle Encyclopedia* are simply enormous, making this encyclopedia all-inclusive. Over 7,000 ancient books were included, which pretty much covered the entire collection in the imperial book agency, Wenyuange, during the Ming Dynasty. The collection there included an array of subjects such as agriculture, art, astronomy, drama, geology, history, literature, medicine, natural sciences, religion, and technology. The result was the creation of a "library" in the early years of the 15th century. Over 500 very rare books have been found in this encyclopedia by later generations. After it was completed, the *Yongle Encyclopedia* was kept in the imperial court and not circulated in print. It was eventually destroyed by a big fire and thefts.

It is estimated that the surviving volumes of the *Yongle Encyclopedia* in libraries and private collections in China total just over 800 rolls and 400-plus volumes, less than 4% of the original.

The Compendium of Works of the Past and the Present

The largest and most complete officially compiled reference book in existence is *The Compendium of Works of the Past and the Present* published during the Qing Dynasty. This book has 10,040 rolls, 5,020 volumes in 525 sheaths and about 170 million characters. It also includes over 10,000 illustrations and 6,000 cited works.

Chen Menglei (1650–1741) and Jiang Tingxi (1669–1732) during the reigns of Kangxi and Yongzheng presided over the editing. Chen Menglei contributed most to this huge project. The editing took 28 years and was completed in 1726. Emperor Yongzheng ordered 65 copies made from copper block type. They were completed in 1728. They were used as gifts for high government officials and not circulated until 1890, when the Shanghai Tongwen Bookstore was commissioned by the inner court to make 100 copies in the original size. These copies were used as gifts to foreign countries.

Adhering to the rules of arrangement for reference books, summarized as "dividing things based on their categories," the overall structure of *The Compendium of Works of the Past and the*

Portrait of Qing Dynasty Emperor Kangxi reading

Binding of *The Compendium of Works of the Past and the Present.*
The interior court copperplate edition of *Illustrations of the Compendium of Works of the Past and the Present* from the reign of Emperor Yongzheng of the Qing Dynasty.

Present is based on a classification system designed on the basis of the traditional cognitive approach of "sky, earth, human, matter and thing," which is formed by *"Huibian," "Dian"* and *"Bu."* With a clear and meticulous category system, it goes far beyond previous reference books and further develops the concept of "dividing things based on their categories." It represents a maturity in the development of ancient China reference books. Therefore, it is hailed as the "Kangxi Encyclopedia" or "Chinese Encyclopedia" by foreigners and has long enjoyed great fame both at home and abroad.

Siku Quanshu and *Revised Continuation of Siku Quanshu*

The compilation of book series started very early. Of all the book series, the one with the largest scale and biggest influence was the *Siku Quanshu*, officially compiled during the Qing Dynasty. The four branches refer to *Jing* classics, *Shi* histories, *Zi* philosophy works and *Ji* anthologies. The collection is complete, intact and diversified.

This enterprise started in 1772 and concluded in 1782. It covers 3,470 ancient books, 79,018 rolls in 36,078 volumes with approximately 1 billion Chinese characters. It is about 44 times as big as the Encyclopedia edited by Diderot. It is so massive and influential that no book to this day can challenge its scale.

Basically, *Siku Quanshu* covered all the most important cultural works of literature before Emperor Qianlong's reign. In terms of coverage and magnitude, it was unprecedented not

Portrait of Emperor Qianlong in court dress

only in China but also in the world. Under the four categories there were sub-categories, including 10 under *Jing*, 15 under *shi*, 14 under *zi*, and 5 under *ji*. In all, there were 44 categories.

During the editing of *Siku Quanshu*, based on the content, times and biographical notes, the origin of the version and other information of the collected book, editors of *The Outline of the Title Catalogue of Siku Quanshu* with 200 volumes, which is the great collection of ancient title catalogues. Its numerous volumes made it difficult to read, so Emperor Qianlong ordered officials to write a concise version of this title catalogue under the name *The Concise Title Catalogue of Siku Quangshu*, which included 20 volumes.

To store *Siku Quanshu*, Emperor Qianlong had seven buildings constructed, modeled after the famous Tianyige in Ningbo. They are collectively called seven chambers in the north and the south. The north libraries are Wenyuange in the Forbidden City,

Handwritten edition of *Literary Essays of the Siku Quanshu* by the Imperial Academy

Wenyuange in the Old Summer Palace, Wensuge in Shenyang, and Wenjin Chamber in the Summer Resort of Chengde. These four imperial libraries were not open to the public.

The three south libraries are Wenlange in Hangzhou, Wenhuige in Yangzhou and Wenzongge in Zhenjiang, which were open to intellectuals for reading and transcribing. Currently four of the seven copies of *Siku Quanshu* are preserved in the China National Library (Wenjinge), Taiwan Library (Wenyuange), Gansu Provincial Library (Wensuge) and Zhejiang Provincial Library (Wenlange). Three other copies were destroyed in war in the 1860s.

The copied books in *Siku Quanshu* have neat handwriting, clear painting and wonderful binding. Books belonging to *Jing, Shi, Zi* and *Ji*—or classical, historical, philosophical, and belles-lettres are covered by silks of different colors. Green, red, blue and grey represent four seasons respectively. Classics were covered by green silk, historical works in red, works of philosophy in blue and belles-lettres in grey. Several volumes of books are stored in a delicate case made of nanmu. The frame of each volume is red with the four characters for *Siku Quanshu* in the middle of the cover. Below the title *Siku Quanshu*, was the name of the copied book, the serial number of the volume and the page number. Each volume has its own summary at the beginning.

It should be pointed out that in the process of compiling *Siku Quanshu*, many books that were regarded harmful to Emperor

Wenlange Tower in Hangzhou Zhejiang, it was the only surviving part of the Nan San Ge.

Qianlong's rule were either deleted or destroyed, which distorted many precious works and simply made them disappear. Still *Siku Quanshu* played some positive roles. On the whole, the completion of *Siku Quanshu* highlighted the ambition of the Chinese nation and wisdom—as well as stigma—of scholars. Arguably, the Great Wall, the Grand Canal, and *Siku Quanshu* are precious parts of China's heritage.

China launched the continuation of *Siku Quanshu* in 1994. All 1,800 volumes have been written and edited over eight years. It was published in 2002 by Shanghai Classics Publishing House. The continuation is a succession of *Siku Quanshu* to arrange and collect large Chinese classics across the country. The collection of *Revised Continuation of Siku Quanshu* includes classics published before and after *Siku Quanshu* went into circulation, that's 5,213 classics, an increase of 51% compared with the original *Siku Quanshu*.

The best edition of each book was chosen as the basis. Following the style of *Siku Quanshu*, the *Revised Continuation of Siku Quanshu* is divided according to *Jing, Shi, Zi* and *Ji* and

Manuscript edition of the *Concise Bibliography of the Siku Quanshu* and its case

categories are marked with the colors green, red, blue and grey. There are 1,800 hardback copies of books printed in A4 format, 260 of which are *Jing* or classical works, 670 *Shi* or historical works, 370 *Zi* or philosophical works and 500 *Ji* or belles-lettres. This book and the original *Siku Quanshu* form a large collection of significant Chinese classics published before 1911.

Poetry Anthologies of People from the Tang Dynasty: *Complete Collection of Tang Poetry* and *Three Hundred Tang Poems*

China is known as the homeland of poetry. Poetry has always been a main form of traditional Chinese literature. Ancient Chinese poetry, or classical Chinese poetry, refers to poetry created by classical Chinese and based on rules and forms of classical poems. In a broad sense, ancient poetry includes many ancient Chinese verses such as *Fu*, *Ci* and *Qu* and so on; while in a narrow sense, it includes ancient-style poetry and "modern style" poetry. Tang Poetry, Song Ci and Yuan Qu respectively represent the greatest accomplishment of literature in different times in thousands of years of poetic history.

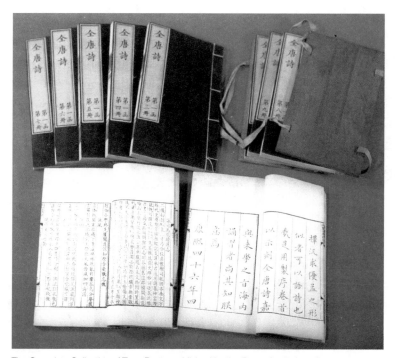

The Complete Collection of Tang Poetry published by the Poetry Institution of Ynagzhou during the reign of Emperor Kangxi of the Qing Dynasty

The Tang Dynasty (618–907) was the most splendid and prosperous time for Chinese ancient poetry. Tang Poetry stands as the pinnacle of ancient Chinese poetry. Based on the conclusions by scholar Cheng Yuzhui, the prosperity of Tang Poetry can be demonstrated by six aspects. First, the quantity of poems produced, at more than 50,000, is unparalleled. Second, Tang poetry included an unprecedented number of poets from a wide range of social classes, many of which are famous. Third, Tang poetry was created from various schools of poetry and focused on a wide range of subjects and styles. Fourth, Tang Poetry consists of different types of poems such as Yue Fu or folk poetry, Wu Jue or classical poems with four five-character lines, Qi Jue or septasyllabic, Wu Lü or classical poem with eight five-character lines, Qi Lü or septasyllabic regulated verse, and so forth. Fifth, Tang poetry includes numerous famous poems. Sixth, Tang Poetry reflects the creative spirit and pursuit of novelty and change.

Famous poets from the Tang Dynasty such as Li Bai, Du Fu, Bai Juyi, Wang Wei and Cen Shen all have extant collections of poems that are widely read and recited by later generations. Most Tang poetry has been collected in the *Complete Collection of Tang Poetry* edited during the Qing Dynasty. This collection is considered a complete collection of Tang Poetry. Since the Tang Dynasty, selected works of Tang poetry have surfaced one after another, the most popular of which is *Three Hundred Tang Poems*, edited by Heng Tang Hermit or Sun Zhu.

The *Complete Collection of Tang Poetry*, the largest collection of the genre, is the complete collection of Tang Poetry works. It was edited in the early years of the Qing Dynasty by Cao Yin, Peng Dingqiu and others on orders from Emperor Kangxi. It contains 900 volumes. According to statistics by Japanese scholar Hiraoka Takeo, there are 49,403 poems and 1,553 *Ju* by 2,873 writers in the *Complete Collection of Tang Poetry*. Editing started in May 1705 and finished in October 1706. The reason why it took such a short time to compile the collection was that scholars from past dynasties made great efforts to keep track of Tang poetry. Cao Yin and other scholars made full use of the achievements of their ancestors. Among these achievements, *Tang Yin Tong Qian* by Hu Zhenheng (1569–1645) from the Ming Dynasty and *Tang Poetry* by Ji Zhenyi (1630–1674) from the beginning of the Qing Dynasty were the most important.

The *Complete Collection of Tang Poetry* was printed and published by the inner court in the years after it was finished. The Poetry Institution of Yangzhou then published it. The two editions both contain 120 volumes and are split into 10 cases. Collecting Tang poetries into one book, the *Complete Collection of Tang Poetry* facilitates study, although there are some flaws in it

The wooden-type print version of *Tangshi Leiyuan* from the reign of Emperor Shenzong of the Ming Dynasty, whose imperial title was Wanli.

due to the speed in which it was collected.

After the publication of this book, many supplements and textual criticisms were published in the later dynasties. Among them, the *Supplement of the Complete Collection of Tang Poetry* published by the Zhonghua Book Company was the most significant. Meanwhile, the complete electronic and a complete network retrieval system for the *Complete Collection of Tang Poetry* has been established to provide convenience to readers.

Three Hundred Tang Poems by Heng Tang Hermit or Sun Zhu is the most popular selected work of Tang poetries. It is the best primer reading material. Heng Tang Hermit original name was Sun Zhu. He was from Wuxi, Jiangsu Province. He was a diligent, studious and incorruptible official. Because he thought there was a shortage of Tang poetry for beginners, he decided to edit a new collection suitable for private schools that could be handed down to later generations. He chose often-quoted and easy-to-read poems.

In 1765, the book was finished. It was based on the styles and times of the poems. There were 310 poems by 77 poets from the Tang Dynasty, 33 of which were Wu Yan or poems with five characters in each line, 46 were Yue Fu or folk poetry, 28 were Qi Yan or poems with seven characters in each line, 50 were Qi Lü or eight-line poems with seven characters per line and following rigorous prosodic rules, 29 were Wu Jue or classical poems with four five-character lines, 51 of which were Qi Jue or septasyllabic. Each of the poems was matched with an explanation and comment.

Opinions about the origin of the book title vary. Some say the title stemmed from a saying which read like this: "If you are familiar with three hundreds Tang poems, you can recite poems even if you cannot compile them." Others say the title originated from *The Book of Odes*. After the book was published, it becomes so popular that almost every family has a copy. It has become the most common book of selected Tang poems that is suitable for everyone and continuously published. For hundreds of years, it has maintained its popularity.

Anthology of Ci of People from the Song Dynasty: *Complete Collection of Song Ci*

Song Ci, another literary genre that appeared after Tang, and Tang Poetry are known as the Two Excellencies of Literature. Both represent the pinnacle of literature from a particular dynasty. In terms of style, Song Ci can be divided into two schools as follows: One is graceful and restrained with Li Qingzhao, Liu Yong and Qin Guan and others as representatives;

the other is bold and unconstrained with Xin Qiji, Su Shi and Chen Liang and others as representatives. The *Complete Collection of Song Ci* is the largest collection of Song Ci edited by contemporary Tang Guizhang.

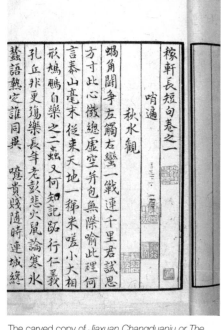

The publication of *The Collection of Sixty Famous Ci writers in The Song Dynasty* by the famous publisher Mao Jin at the end of the Ming Dynasty marked the beginning of the edition and printing of collections of *ci* writers in the Song Dynasty. After that, different collections by other editors in later dynasties were published. However, none of them could give the whole picture of the Song *Ci*.

The carved copy of *Jiaxuan Changduanju or The Collection of Ci* by Xin Qiji published by Guangxin Book House in 1299

In the 1930s, on the basis of different collections by different editors, Tang Guizhang collected and started to compile the *Complete Collection of Song Ci*. After sever years of hard work, his collection was finished and Commercial Press published a thread-bound edition in 1940. After the founding of the PRC, Tang Guizhang started the supplement and revision of his book and Zhonghua Book Company published a new edition in 1965.

There are more than 1,400 *ci* included as supplements in the new edition whose style is different from that of the old one. In the old edition, *ci* are arranged according to the classification of "Emperor" and "imperial clan"; while in the new one, it is arranged based on time with an index of authors at the end of the book. There are 20,000 *ci* by 1,330 writers from the Southern Song Dynasty and Northern Song Dynasty with more than 530

The portrait of Tang Guizhang

reference books.

After the publication of this new edition, the editor kept revising and supplementing the book and *The Supplement and Revision* was added to the end of the reprinted version of this book in 1979. In all, with a complete collection and careful revision and edition, this book is a must among reference books of Song Ci research. Tang Guizhang, who accomplished the edition and completed the collection of Song Ci along, set an outstanding example in the history of Chinese modern edition and publishing history.

Collections of Yuan Qu: *The Complete Collection of Yuan Sanqu* and *The Anthology of Yuan Qu*

With unique style in thought, content and of high artistic level, Yuan Qu is an exquisite piece of Chinese literature. It is on a par with Tang Poetry and Song *Ci*. As the main part of literature from the Yuan Dynasty, Yuan Qu, which contains *Zaju* and *Sanqu*, was not only literature for the educated and officials to express their feeling and ambitions but also a brand new artistic style popular among average people. There are numerous writers of Yuan Qu, among who are Guan Hanqing, Tang Xianzhu and Ji Junxiang. Their masterpieces are *Dou E's Grievance, West Chamber, The Little Orphan of the House of Chao* as their masterpieces, which enjoy a high reputation in literary circles around the world.

The most famous selected work is *The Anthology of Yuan Qu* edited by Zang Maoxun (1550–1620) during the Ming Dynasty. It collects 100 different kinds of Yuan Dramas in 100 volumes. The book is also known as *One Hundred Qu of Yuan People*. The number of extant Yuan Drama by Yuan people includes less than 200 kinds and more than half of them are collected in *The Anthology of Yuan Qu* which focuses on well-known plays, such as *Dou E's Grievance* by Guan Hanqing, *Emperor Minghuang of Tang Dynasty and the Phoenix Tree in a Rainy Night in Autumn* by Bai Pu and *The Autumn in Han Palace* by Ma Zhiyuan and so on by different play writers.

Therefore, with its great influence, this book plays a significant role in the spread of Yuan Drama. Sui Shusen, a contemporary scholar, collected Yuan *Zaju* found during the past decades and compiled "*The Supplement of the Anthology of Yuan Qu*," which was published by Zhonghua Book Company in September 1959. In the above two books, *The Anthology of Yuan Qu* and *The Supplement of The Anthology of Yuan Qu*, all extant Yuan Dramas are collected.

The Anthology of Yuan Qu, edited by Sui Shushen in the contemporary era, is the most famous complete collection of Yuan Sanqu. It includes works from 213 authors, from Yuan Haowen of the Jin Dynasty to Gu Zijing at the end of the Yuan Dynasty and several anonymous works. There are over 3,800 *Xiaoling*, 450 *Taoqu* arranged in the authors' chronological sequence. With a short biography for each author and the source of each work, it provides a whole picture of the *Sanqu* in the Yuan Dynasty. Among the 6 volumes of *White Snow in Early Spring*

collected by Luo Zhenyu and found recently by the library of Liaoning Province, there are 25 unseen *Tao Qu*, which can be the supplement of *The Anthology of Yuan Qu*.

Novels in the Ming and Qing Dynasties: *"Four Great Classical Novels"* and *"Three Collections and Short Stories"*

The Ming and Qing dynasties were periods of prosperity for Chinese classical fiction. Novels from the Ming and Qing dynasties have unprecedented scope and depth. They mirror the various aspects of the social life at the time and became an important literary genre for people to understand their social environment and entertain themselves. In Chinese literary history, they are considered parallel to Tang Poetry, Song Ci and Yuan Qu. Among them, the famous "Four Great Classical Novels," namely *Romance of the Three Kingdoms, Pilgrimage to the West, Water Margin* and *A Dream of Red Mansions*, are precious cultural heritage.

Romance of The Three Kingdoms has 120 chapters and is based on *The History of The Three Kingdoms* by Chen Shou combined with the folk tales. Luo Guanzhong completed it at the end of the Yuan Dynasty and the early Ming Dynasty (1330–1400). As the first Zhanghui-style novel in China, it has plain text, numerous impressive figures, an intricate plot and a vast narrative structure. It vividly describes the complicated military and political struggles among the Wei, Shu and Wu kingdoms during the end of the Eastern Han Dynasty and the Three Kingdoms Period.

Water Margin, by Shi Naian (1296–1371) or by Shi Naian and Luo Guanzhong, based on *Xuanhe Yishi* (a story book), depicts a majestic story of 108 people led by Song Jiang who are driven to revolt during the North Song Dynasty. As the first demotic oral-language novel in China, the novel, with intricate plots, vivid description and characters, has a very high artistic value and a high place in literary history. The book has spread and spawned a variety of versions, some with 100 chapters, others with 120 and others with 70.

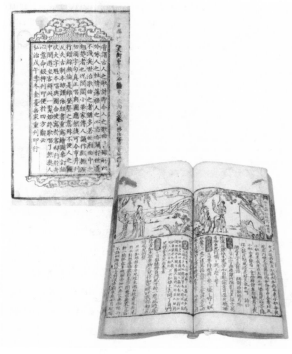

Pilgrimage to the West has 100 chapters and is based on the related story scripts of *Zaju* and the folklore of Xuanzang's going on a pilgrimage for the Buddhist

Jintai Yue's carving copy of *Qimiao Quanxiang Xixiangji* published by Beijing Book House in 1498

Scriptures. It was written by Wu Cheng'en (about 1504–1582) during the Ming Dynasty. The first seven chapters of the book deal with plots about the Monkey King such as "Monkey King being born," "Making havoc in Heaven" and others. The other chapters in the story deal with vanquished demons and monsters and overcoming difficulties in a pilgrimage for the Buddhist Scriptures with his three disciples Monkey King, Pigsy and Monk Sha. The book, very creative, with romantic descriptions, humorous language, large scope and complete structure, is a unique and outstanding piece of colloquial fiction.

A Dream of Red Mansions by the great writer Cao Xueqin (1715–1763) from the Qing Dynasty, takes the writer's family life as an archetype and with the love and marriage tragedy among Chia Pao-yu, Lin Dai-yu and Xue Baochai as its main plot, tracks the rise and fall of the prominent Chia family and reveals the inevitable collapse and end of feudal society and the beginnings of democracy. The book, with a well-knit plot, real life detail and an elegant language as well as a colorful and diverse content, an intricate plot, profound ideological thought and an exquisite artistic skill, is the greatest realistic work in ancient Chinese novels. The present popular version of the book has 120 chapters, the first 80 chapters of which were written by Cao Xueqin and the rest by Gao E.

The most outstanding colloquial short stories in the Ming and Qing dynasties are the *Three Collections and Short Stories*, namely *Yushimingyan*, *Jingshitongyan* and *Xingshihengyan* by

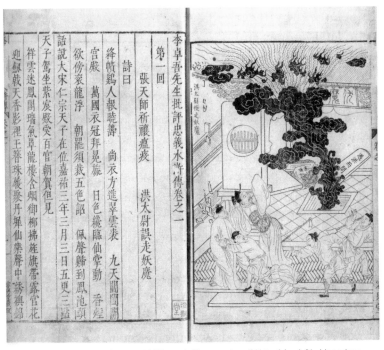

The Rongyutang's carved copy of *Li Zuowu's Comment on "Water Margin"* in Hangzhou from the reign of Shenzong of the Ming Dynastry, whose imperial title was Wanli

Feng Menglong (Three Collections) as well as *Chuke Pai'an jingqi* and *Erke Pai'an jingqi* by Ling Mengchu (The Short Stories).

The former, with 120 selected scripts and story scripts, taken from unofficial history or legends, from the Song, Ming and Qing dynasties, reflects city residents' thought, life and interests and greatly influences the later colloquial fictions and dramas. Thanks to the writer, the latter, with 40 story scripts for each

A Dream of Red Mansions published by the Zhonghua Book Company

and inferior to *Three Collections* in ideological content and artistic quality, integrates standards and language style.

The *Strange Tales of a Lonely Studio,* an outstanding representative book of classic Chinese novels in the Ming and Qing dynasties by Pu Songling of the Qing Dynasty, includes 491 short stories, abundant subject matters and diverse content, most of which vigorously criticizes the darkness and corruption of the society at the time through stories about fox spirits and ghosts. The book, with bright and vivid figures and complicated and eccentric plots, successfully builds up numerous model personalities. Bearing the features of a tightly knit structure, a well-organized layout, a succinct style and a minute description, it can be rated as a peak work in ancient Chinese short stories.

Encyclopedia of China

Chinese cultural circles have been always followed the fine tradition of compiling reference books. After the introduction of the modern encyclopedia, Chinese scholars, with several small and practical encyclopedias compiled in the early 20th century, took the compiling of a modern encyclopedia as an object of their endeavors.

In 1978, the State Council decided to edit and publish the *Encyclopedia of China* and set up the Encyclopedia of China Publishing House to lead the work. By 1993, 74 volumes of all disciplines, with 126 million words, nearly 50 thousand pictures in 780 thousand entries, had been published. As a famous first edition, the *Encyclopedia of China*, is available for readers above the senior high school or college level education. Its publication was hailed as "a monument of Chinese Culture" and it became a well-developed and prosperous symbol of Chinese scientific and

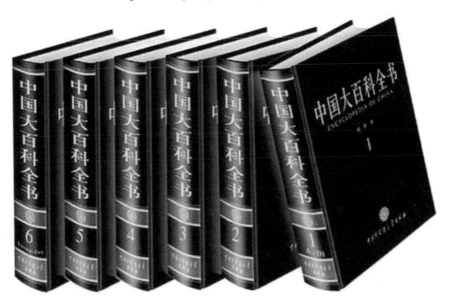

The first edition of *Encyclopedia of China*

cultural undertakings.

According to common international practice, a new edition of the encyclopedia usually comes out at several-year intervals. Since the first edition of the *Encyclopedia of China*, abrupt changes have taken place in society, which result in the need to constantly update knowledge in various fields. In this connection, the edition and publishing work of the second edition of *Encyclopedia of China* was in place in 1995. After more than 10 years of work by the editorial committee and scholars around the country, the second edition was finished and published by Encyclopedia of China Publishing House.

Based on the first edition, the second edition of *Encyclopedia of China*, adapted to the development and demands of the era, has had numerous entries edited, replaced and renewed. Entries have been classified and similar entries combined while staple entries have been preserved, improves the original.

With a total of 32 volumes (30 volumes of text and 2 for the index), 60 million words, 30,000 pictures and nearly 1,000 maps and 60 thousand entries, the second edition, is accurate, authoritative, readable and easily and quickly accessible. It is a systematic and comprehensive reflection of the latest developments in science and provides abundant reflection of significant achievements in the process of building socialism with Chinese characteristics. In addition, it is not only a set of practical reference books suited to public reading and use but also serves the economic and social development and is the first set large-scale modern comprehensive encyclopedia in China that conforms to common international practices in China.

The Progressive Vicissitude
The Modernization of China's Publishing Industry

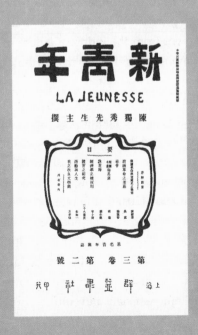

At the beginning of the 19th century, advanced publishing technology was introduced to China, heralding a profound transformation in Chinese publishing. After the Opium War in 1840, developed capitalist countries from Europe and America broke China's self-seclusion. At the same time, with the influence of capitalism, traditional Chinese society began to collapse with modernization as the keynote for future development. During the tremendous changes society and culture underwent, the traditional publishing industry was left behind the times and started its modernization, entering into a transition period. What's more, the period marked a move for the Chinese publishing industry from tradition to modernity, gradually establishing a solid foundation for modernization.

At the end of the 19th century and beginning of the 20th, a large group of modern private publishing agencies such as Commercial Press, Zhonghua Publishing House and Wenming Publishing House emerged. They symbolized the end of the transition for Chinese publishing industry from traditional to modern. From that time forward, the modern publishing industry became the mainstay and was markedly different from the industry before the 19th century. The differences in modern publishing match the development of Chinese society.

On the whole, the 100 years from the beginning of Opium war in 1840 to the founding of the People's Republic of China was a significant stage for the rise and development of modern Chinese publishing. The period from the beginning of the 20th century to 1949 was particularly prosperous. According to conservative estimates, from 1911 to 1949, at least 120,000 different books were published in China. There were more than 10,000 periodicals and magazines and 2,500 newspapers. The sheer number of publications was unprecedented in China's publishing history. Meanwhile, the rise of a modern publishing industry played an active role in promoting the development of Chinese society and culture.

The Introduction and Application of Mechanical Printing

The introduction of modern printing technology from the west facilitated the rise of modern Chinese publishing. By the early years of the 19th century, mechanized letterpress printing had been introduced in China and the Christian Protestant missionary Robert Morrison (1782–1834) from the London Missionary Society brought the first Chinese character font set to China. In 1814, he founded a printing shop in Malacca to cut matrixes of Chinese characters and cast types out of them. In 1819, a printed Chinese copy of *The Holy Bible—the Old Testament and the New Testament* was the first Chinese printed book and resulted in the first group of trained press operators.

Since the 1840 Opium War, western missionaries came to China and some of them began to do printing and publishing

Large electric printing machine used in the Zhonghua Book House at the beginning of 20th century

to facilitate their missionary work. In 1843, British missionary Walter Henry Medhurst (1796–1857) moved his printing shop from Batavia to Shanghai and named it Mohai Book House. It was the first printing and publishing agency with letterpress printing machines in Shanghai. After the founding of the Mohai Book House, a number of publishing agencies set up by foreigners emerged, including Meihua Book House, Yinghua Book House and Gezhi Book House. The largest was Meihua, which also had the most publications and most advanced technology.

In 1879, a British businessman named Ernest Major (1830–1908) founded the Dianshizai Printing House to print Chinese books by polyqutography. The books printed by Dianshizhai were portable and popular, small in size with beautiful scripts and low prices. After that, polyautography became popular and a number of polyautography book houses were set up. Polyautography replaced block-printing as the most common printing form in China and helped set up profit driven printing agencies.

At the beginning of the 20th century, polyautography was replaced by type printing as the use of printing machines spread. Improvements and innovations were made for the new type of printing based on the unique features of Chinese characters. After than, developing by leaps and bounds, printing technology in China narrowed the distance with technology used in western countries and moved from manual operation to

British missionary Robert Morrison, a missionary and pioneer translator

Shanghai's Dianshizhai Printing House drawn by Wu Youru, a famous Qing Dynasty painter

mechanization.

After developing for almost 100 years from the beginning of the 19th century to the 20th century, modern machine printing became the mainstream of China's printing industry. Traditional printing technologies such as movable-type printing or block-printing and registration printing were left behind. With these fundamental changes in productivity, the printing industry gradually became an industrial enterprise and adopted capitalist operating models.

The transition to modern printing directly led to the transition of the traditional Chinese book system. Before the 19th century, thread-bound books were the most common in China. After the introduction of new printing technologies, paper imported from abroad also emerged. Statistics show that in 1903, the value of paper imported from abroad hit 2,684,000 taels of silver. By 1911, the value had jumped to 5,605,000 taels. From 1903 to 1911, a total of 34,165,000 taels of silver were spent to import paper. As a result, imported paper replaced cork paper and became the most commonly used. It also allowed for a shift from one-side printing to printing on both sides of the page.

In addition, there changes in binding and layout as western styles overtook most publications. Popular in the west, hardcover and paper cover books began to be widely used in China, marking a transformation in book binding and layout.

The Rise of New Publishing Houses

After the 19th century, the traditional publishing system started to decline and collapse. At the same time, modern profit-driven publishing houses emerged, developed and promoted the development and reform of society in unprecedented ways.

Missionaries and foreign merchants set up publishing agencies with capitalist features. These enterprises provided examples and guided the modernization of China's publishing industry. The most famous were the Mohai Book House, Yinghua Book House, Meihua Book House, The Christian Literature Society for China and the Shanghai Newspaper Press, among others. These publishing agencies used advanced publishing strategies, technology and management from the west and promoted the transition of China's publishing from traditional to modern.

After the rise of the "Westernization Movement" in the 1860s, influenced by new publishing agencies of the west, the Qing Dynasty government established translation schools and official book bureaus comprising of the Translation Department of the Jiangnan Arsenal, the Beijing Translation School, The Jinling Book House, the Zhejiang Book House, the Jiangsu Book House and so on. These new organizations were markedly different from the traditional official publishing industry.

Modern web press that uses different types of paper

From the end of the 19th century to the early years of the 20th century, the general mood of society in China changed and private publishing agencies emerged. In 1882, Xu Hongfu and Xu Run set up the Tongwen Book House in Shanghai, the first private modern publishing enterprise founded by Chinese with private funds. After that, a group of private modern publishing enterprises like the Feiying School, Hongwen Book House and Jishi Book House emerged. At the same time, some traditional private book houses changed themselves into modern publishing agencies.

The founding of Commercial Press in 1897 marked a new development stage in China's modern private publishing. In 1906, the first book industry chamber of commerce was set up in Shanghai with 22 new publishing agencies as members. After the founding of Commercial Press, many new private publishing agencies sprung up such as Zhonghua Book House, Civilization Book House, World Books, Dadong Book House and Kaiming Book House. Market-oriented and guided by modern publishing concepts, these book houses used modern machine-printing and resorted to various and flexible modern operation models to fulfill their social responsibility as publishers while maximizing their commercial profits. They became the mainstay of modern Chinese publishing and led to a new prosperity in modern Chinese publishing.

Among the numerous private publishing agencies, Commercial Press and Zhonghua Book House are the most influential and have the longest history. In 1936, 9,438 books were published and republished. Of those, Commercial Press published 4,938 and Zhonghua Book House 1,548. These two presses published 6,486 books or 69% of all the books in the country.

Commercial Press and Zhang Yuanji

Commercial Press was established by Xia Ruifang, Bao Xian'en, Bao Xianchang and Gao Fengchi and others in Dechangli, Jiangxi Road in Shanghai in 1897. At the beginning of the 20th century, in step with the New Culture Movement that advocated vernacular writings, Commercial Press set up new publications, edited and published many books about new thoughts and emerging culture. Besides introducing western learning and publishing versions of Chinese classics, Commercial Press also edited and published many textbooks and copies of ancient books. More importantly it trained plenty of editorial staff that went on to found or lead some famous publishing agencies early in the 20th century. Commercial Press went from being a small printing house to become the largest new publishing enterprise in the history of modern China, mostly thanks to the leadership of Zhang Yuanji.

Zhang Yuanji (1867–1959) was originally from Zhejiang

Province. He was a famous sinologist, historian and the most influential publisher in modern history. In 1920, at the invitation by Xia Ruifang, Zhang Yuanji joined Commercial Press. He regarded the development of education as his duty.

In 1903, He took over the post of director of the communication and translation institution of Commercial Press. He took over as manager in 1916. By 1926 he had become president of the press, a post he held until his death. During his 50-year publishing career, Zhang Yuanji made outstanding contributions to the modern publishing industry, culture and education.

As a great publisher with groundbreaking ideas and well versed in both Chinese and western cultures, Zhang Yuanji was erudite, well-informed and insightful with daring and resolution as well as strong patriotic passion and a sense of social responsibility. Taking advantage of the emergence of new learning and the abolishment of the imperial civil examination system by the Qing Government, he formed a team to write and

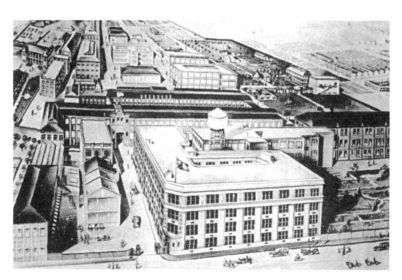

A restored modern panorama of Commercial Press, which grew rapidly and became the largest press in the Far East in the 20th century.

Zhang Yuanji

The title page of *Ideal Textbook*, part of a series published by Commercial Press

edit new textbooks.

Under Zhang Yuanji's leadership, the first textbook for primary school was published in 1904. The book broke new ground in the history of modern Chinese education. After that first effort, textbooks published by Commercial Press became popular across the country. Zhang Yuanji also devoted himself to introducing western cultures and bringing new knowledge into China. He carefully chose and organized the translation and publication of a large group of academic and literary classics from abroad. Among them, the *Origin of the Species* translated by Yan Fu (1854–1921)and *La dame aux camellias* translated by Lin Shu, which had profound influence.

He also set up the East Library and the Hanfenlou Library and made use of the resources in more than 50 official or private libraries to print 610 books and 20,000 volumes by photo-offset, including *Sibucongkan*, *The Histories of Twenty-four Dynasties* and

Xuguyi Series. Beautifully printed, these unprecedented versions were complete and became examples for later generations. The Commercial Press also edited and published lots of reference books. In 1915, the first new dictionary *Ci Yuan* or *Chinese Etymological Dictionary* was published. The press also published many well-known periodicals such as *The Magazine of the East*, *Novel Monthly*, *Education*, *Women*, *Students* and others.

During the Second World War, Commercial Press was destroyed. Zhang Yuanji formed a committee to revive the press and wrote a slogan that underlined his enthusiasm, and that of the country's, for new publishing ventures: "Sacrificing for the country and striving for culture." He continued printing in Chongqing and other places.

Zhonghua Book House and Lu Feikui

In the history of modern Chinese publishing, the Zhonghua Book House, established in 1912, enjoys equal fame to the Commercial Press. Its founder was Lu Feikui, who was from Zhejiang Province. He was well educated and had plenty of

An institution of the Zhonghua Book House

publishing experience. He led the Zhonghua Book House for almost 30 years, during which time the book house published more than 4,000 different books.

In its first year of operation in 1912, fixed capital was only 25,000 RMB. By 1916, the printing house's capital had reached 1,600,000 RMB and the book house became the second largest private press in the country, behind Commercial Press.

The house had a number of significant types of publications. Textbooks were the most

Textbooks published by Zhonghua Book House

important. The publishing house put out more than 400 different textbooks, which were the best in the industry in the years of the Republic of China. The second most important type was social science books. There were more than one thousand different social science books edited and published by the book house. Among them, *Culture Series*, *Social Science Series* and so on were most popular. The third type was magazines. The book house published more than 20 magazines, among which *The Great Zhonghua*, *Education in Zhonghua*, *Novels in Zhonghua*, *Students in Zhonghua*, *Children in Zhonghua*, *Women in Zhonghua*, *Zhonghua English Weekly* and *Zhonghua Children Pictorial* were most famous. The fourth type was reference books. The *Zhonghua Great Dictionary* was published in 1915, *The Compendium of Works of Past and Present* printed by photo-offset and *Words Encyclopedia* published in 1936 were the most famous. The fifth type was ancient books, which were rearranged and reprinted. *The Ju*

Zhen Fang Song Version of the Histories of Twenty-four Dynasties published in 1930 and the Ju Zhen Fang Song version of *Si Bu Bei Yao* printed in 1930 were best known.

The Emergence of New Publications

After the 19th century, with the rise of modern publishing, the content and type of publications in China changed greatly.

Books focused on modern disciplines

Confucian classics, history, philosophy, literature are the main categories of Chinese traditional books. After the 1840s, China opened up to the outside world gradually with increasing contacts with the west. As a result, intellectuals broadened their horizons and began to learn about and introduce western culture and thoughts. At the same time, many translated books were published to spread the new knowledge, which led to fundamental changes in the content and structure of publications. Besides Confucian classics, many books on history, philosophy, literature, many natural sciences, applied science, philosophy

Chinese scholar Hua Hengfang (1833–1902) and his translated version of *Elements of Geology*, which was different from traditional works on geography.

147

and social science were published and many new disciplines established. More than 120,000 different books in 18 categories published from 1912 to 1949 were collected in *The Title Catalogue in the Years of the Republic of China*, comprising philosophy, psychology, religion, politics, law, military, economy, culture, science, education, sports, literature, arts, medicine and health, agricultural science, communication, transportation and others. Based on these classifications, by 1949, the system of modern disciplines had become almost mature.

Newspapers and magazines published in massive scale

With the great expansion of content for publication, the types of Chinese publications were enriched increasingly and various new publications came into existence. Newspapers and magazines are published in a large scale. *The Join Title Catalogue of Chinese periodicals of China* shows almost 20,000 Chinese periodicals in 50 libraries across China, which were published at home and abroad from 1833 to 1949. *The catalogue of Collected Chinese newspapers published before the founding of PRC in Shanghai*

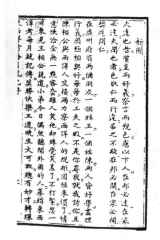
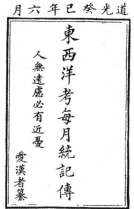

The first Chinese periodical set up in 1833 in Mainland China. It was called *East and West Study Monthly.*

Library records more than 3,500 different Chinese newspapers, published at home and abroad from 1862 to 1949. According to these two figures, the state of the newspapers and magazines publishing industry can be ascertained. In addition to reporting the news, those modern newspapers and magazines promoted the development of modern publishing and mass media and exerted great influence on society.

Textbooks, new references and pictorial books

From translating versions of foreign textbooks to editing and writing by Chinese, from textbooks of writing in classical Chinese to those of writing in vernacular, from imperfections in style and content to relative perfect editions, textbooks experienced a process of continuous transformations to meet the needs of the times. This evolution was partly based on the sheer variety of publications, including traditional books, category books and title catalogues, as well as a group of references publications edited and published quickly such as newspapers and periodicals indexes, dictionaries, tables, chorographic maps, annuals and handbooks. Pictorials were created on the basis of novels with illustrated portraits of the main characters—pictures were more important than words. These new publications were popular among readers and accepted by society as soon as they were published.

The Social Transition Promoted by New Publishing

Modern ideas filter into people's minds

From the 19th century, during the modernization of Chinese publishing, publishing concepts from the west were introduced into China as western learning spread eastward. The concept of

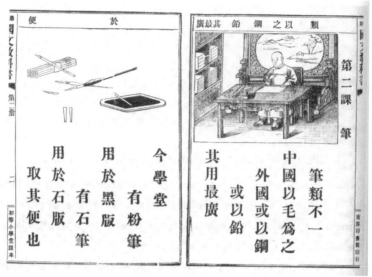

The text from the *Latest Version of Chinese Textbook for Primary School*, printed in the early 20th century by Commercial Press.

"freedom of the press" was one of the most important.

In 1644, the idea of freedom of the press was first proposed in *Areopagitica*, written by British political commentator John Milton. A rising capitalist class used the slogan "freedom of the press" as a weapon to strive for democracy and against feudalistic autocracy. Something similar happened in China. From the mid-1800s, freedom of the press not only became a weapon to criticize and fight against feudalism, but also an ideal and a pursuit for reformists from the capitalist class. In 1912, after the success of the revolution of 1911, the government of the newly founding Republic of China declared in *"The Provisional Constitution of the Republic of China"* that "people enjoy freedom of speech, writing, press, assembly and association," meaning that freedom of the press was a right protected by law.

Different magazines focusing on western learning published in China towards the end of the 19th century.

Dian Shi Zhai Pictorial published in 1887 read: "A crowd of people were looking on a giant from the west."

The establishment of copyright

The concept of the copyright protection gradually made its way to the hearts of people, promoting the establishment of a modern copyright system and the promulgation of copyright law. In 1903, Commercial Press signed the first modern publishing contract in modern China with famous translator Yan Fu for publishing his translation *A General Theory of Society*. The contract read that both the translator and the publisher shared the copyright of this book. If the contract became invalid, the copyright would be left with the translator. The translator could not allow other publishers to print this translation work unless the contract became null and void. Both the translator and the publisher's rights and obligations were specifically identified by the contract that bounded and protected both sides, facilitating the enforcement of the copyright contract, which was originally devoid of substance.

The establishment of the copyright system in the early years of the 20th century not only meant that Chinese writers could enjoy their due rewards, but also shows the acknowledgement and respect for writers' rights held by society at large. Laying the economic foundation for the growth of professional writers, the copyright system directly promoted an increase in the number of writers and allowed for the continuous prosperity of publishing and cultural causes.

The promotion and development of society

Society was a relative closed and stable in China before the 19th century. Although some changes had taken place due to the introduction of Buddhism and western learning that came to China in the end of the Ming Dynasty, no fundamental transformations had taken place, indicating the smooth and slow transition of traditional Chinese culture. This feature exerted profound influence on traditional Chinese publishing, which developed in a closed but stable way.

After the 19th century, a dramatic transformation took place in China due to the influence from foreign countries and a tendency towards modernization. Under these conditions, China's publishing industry was forced to begin its modernization and became a barometer for the fate of the country and its people. In the course of this transition, ideas such as "save the country from doom and strive for national salvation" and "advance with the times" were given priority by the publishing industry. Lots of books on modern natural science and social science were published to spread new thoughts and scientific knowledge, which provided a strong impetus for the development and transformation of Chinese society.

At that time, four types of publications exerted a positive influence on Chinese society. The first was reading material to spread modern scientific and cultural knowledge through

New Youth magazine, which published "A Study on Sport" by Mao Zedong in his youth.

new textbooks and new translations. The second was works to publicize the revolution among people. Third was culture and artistic reading material to elevate people's souls and enrich their lives. The last type was ancient books and other references book to inherit, accumulate and carry the national cultural heritage.

After the 1840s, through the publication of books and magazines, different social classes and parties publicized their political ideas and various advanced cultural and scientific ideas from the west spread through these books. It can be said without exaggeration that the significant political movements in this period and the introduction of western culture in large scale were closely connected with publishing activities, which served as a catalysts in social transformation.

For example, the works translated by the well-known modern translator Yan Fu caused a sensation with the idea of "survival of the fittest in natural selection" influenced several generations. During the early years of the 20th century, a set of books used to publicize the revolution was published to meet the needs of the times. They contributed to the success of the Revolution of 1911. The spread of advanced ideas such as democracy and science published in some publications including *New Youth* could be credited for facilitating the rise of the New Culture Movement in 1919.

Thanks to the interaction between publishing and society, both changed and evolved, laying a solid foundation for the development of contemporary publishing and cultural causes. However, it is necessary to note that, although traditional publishing is no longer in popular use, it did not die out with the advent of modern publishing, It is still visible in some cases and its contributions to Chinese publishing should not be ignored.

Carrying Forward the Cause and Forging into the Future
The Prosperity of Chinese Publishing in the Contemporary Era

From the founding of the People's Republic of China in 1949, as an important part in the great cause of socialism with Chinese characteristics, Chinese publishing made remarkable accomplishments in the continuous development and transformation in its 60-year development history. With the deepening of reforms and opening-up to the outside world, Chinese publishing has become one of the core forces in the cause of socialist culture with Chinese characteristics and culture playing a more and more significant role in the construction of the economy and culture as well as in cultural exchanges between home and abroad. The achievements made during the past 60 years prove that China has become a world-class publishing power and developed momentum emphasized by the splendid accomplishments of ancient publishing.

The Scale of Publication has Enlarged Yearly and Publishing Strength Increased Quickly

Since the founding of the PRC, publishing in the mainland has made great strides, although it has experienced some twists and turns and been affected by some negative elements. Especially after the adoption of reforms and opening-up to the outside world in 1978, Chinese publishing made outstanding achievements best illustrated by the following statistics: In 1950, there were 211 publishing houses across the country and 12,153 books were published with total print runs of 275 million. In 1978, there were 105 presses and 14,987 books were published with the total print runs of 3.774 billion. In 2008, there were 579 publishing houses that put out 274,123 books, 7.062 billion volumes and 56.113 billion actual pieces.

The number of periodicals has increased from over 600 in 1977 to 9,549 in 2008, while that of newspapers has increased from 200 in the past to nearly 1943 in 2008 with 44.292 billion pieces. Circulation numbers for audio-visual products and electronic publications in 1978 was over 30 million pieces; while in 2008, 11,721 audio products were published in 254 million boxes; 11,772 video recording were published in 179 million boxes; the number of electronic publications published hit 9,668 with 157,706,400 units. The Chinese publishing industry has already achieved a historic shift from a shortage of cultural output to a surplus, from a single medium to diverse forms that meet people's various and multi-layered spiritual and cultural needs.

China's publishing industry has made great contributions to the economic development of the country and has had great social benefits. According to statistics from the General Administration of Press and Publication in 2004, the added value of the publishing industry was RMB193.97 billion, accounting for 1.7% of GDP in 2004 and 5% of the added value of the tertiary-

Children choose books at the Xinhua Book Store on the eve of Child's Day.

industry. In 2008, the total price value of books and periodicals reached RMB129.68 billion, the sale value of publications was RMB162.28 billion and total sales for the printing industry surpassed RMB97.69 billion.

In addition, according to prediction made by the research group of the Chinese Institution of Publishing Science in "*A Study on the Development Index System of the Publishing Industry in a Well-off Society*," by 2020, the added value of the Chinese publishing industry will reach RMB800 billion, accounting for 1.9%–2.0% of GDP. Therefore, publishing has become a significant part of the national economy, playing a more and more important part in the promotion of economic and social development.

Concretely, the strength of presses in China has grown with the development of publishing groups. There are currently some 25 publishing groups in China. They have become the most organized producers of published materials in Chinese

The well-known author of many best-sellers Yi Zhongtian shook hands with young readers in his signature court. More than three million volumes of his *Comment on the Three Kingdoms* have been sold.

publishing history. In 2006, publishing groups put out more than 40% of the total number of books printed and accounted for more than 30% of the value of all books sold and 30% of the total number of books published in China. The books published by publishing groups account for over one third of all books published in China, which indicate that publishing groups have become the most important force in the development of Chinese publishing. Meanwhile, among the many publishing groups, the most powerful, the China Publishing Group, represents the development level of Chinese publishing in the contemporary era.

Aiming to meet the needs of reform and development of the publishing industry, the China Publishing Group, a national large-scale publishing institution, was established on April 9th, 2002 with China Publishing Group as the parent company. The company is made up of 14 subsidiary including the People's Literature Publishing House, the Commercial Press, Zhonghua Book Company, Encyclopedia of China Publishing House, China Fine Arts Publishing Group, People's Music Publishing House, SDX Joint Publishing Company, China Translation and Publishing Corporation, Oriental Publishing Center, Modern Education Press, Xinhua Bookstore Head Office, China National Publications Import & Export (Group) Corporation, China Book Business Report and Rongbao Zhai Press. It contains holding companies, mutual shareholding companies and affiliated companies including Zhongxinlian Corporation, Zhongbanlian Corporation, Digital Media Company of China Publishing Group. The Group is a large-scale enterprise that integrates publishing and marketing, chain-operations, import and export trade, copyright trade, printing and reproduction, information technology services, scientific research and development and fundraising, participate in national publishing plans, national publishing awards, the retail market for books, mass publication

The exhibition area of the China Publishing Group during the 16th Beijing International Book Fair in 2009.

sales, export and import of publications and so on.

With 9,800 employees, the group has total capital of RMB6.5 billion and sales income of RMB3.9 billion per year. It turus out more than 10,000 kinds of publications including books, audio-visual products, electronic and online publications as well as 47 types of periodicals and newspapers every year. It has a 7% market share in the domestic publication retail market and makes more than 1,000 copyright deals every year.

The group, the country's largest import and export publication company, exports and imports more than 200,000 various publications every year, accounting for 62% and 30% of the trade in books and periodicals respectively. The group also owns 27 overseas presses, book chain stores and administration bodies with business in more than 130 countries.

Publishing Technology Advances and the Rapid Development of Digital Publishing

In terms of the history of publishing, the progress of the industry has been driven by reforms and transformations in publishing and printing technology. Since the 1980s, advances in Chinese publishing and printing have narrowed the gap with the most advanced in the world and have given momentum to the development of contemporary Chinese publishing.

In July 1981, the first computer of China, Chinese character laser editing and composing system Huaguang I went through appraisal at the ministry-level. Chinese character laser editing and composing technology helped the Chinese publishing industry enter into the new age of "light and electricity" and end the age of "lead and fire." Its inventor Wang Xuan has been

Wang Xuan (1937–2006), the inventor of the Chinese characters laser editing and composing system.

praised as the "Bi Sheng of modern China." (Bi Sheng was the inventor of movable-type printing technology in ancient China.)

After that, laser editing and composing technology was upgraded and color laser editing and composing invented. Due to the system's technology and price, 99% of presses and printing factories in Mainland China use it. Since 1991, presses in Hong Kong, Macao and Taiwan have also used it, including Ta Kun Pao of Hong Kong, the Macao Daily News and Taiwan's Central Daily News. This system has also been introduced to other countries such as Malaysia, the US, Canada, Thailand and Japan. The system allows for faster composition and production of Chinese publishing, saves manpower, financial and material resources and facilitates the digitalization of the entire publishing process and lays a foundation Chinese publishing to keep up with its overseas counterparts.

The rise of new media technologies, such as internet

Digital readers exhibited during the Frankfurt Book Fair in 2009.

networks and mobile phones, provides a sound environment for the development of Chinese digital publishing. By the end of September 2009, there were 360 million internet users in China, a popularization rate of 27.1%. The number of users of mobile internet was 192 million and 99.33 million people used broadband internet. The expansion of basic Internet resources saw the number of IP addresses hit 123 million, the second largest in the world. Total domain name registrations were the highest in the world at 5 million.

In terms of the scale of the market, in 2008, the output value of the internet industry was nearly RMB150 billion. The output value of IT, production, software and the digital industries was RMB200 billion. According to the statistics, in 2009, the total number of mobile phone users exceeded 700 million.

With plenty of new media equipment available, most literate people have the necessary terminals to read new media with products such as the Apabi Reader by the Founder Company, the Hanwang E-Book and Chinese On-line E-Book. These digital publications have large reader groups and market share.

Over the past few years, the scale of digital publishing has grown with an improved industrial chain and various publishing forms. As network and digital reading become important reading forms, e-book, publishing on demand, mobile phone publishing and blogs begin to play an important role in Chinese publishing. In 2002, the value of digital publishing was RMB1.59 billion; by 2008, it had multiplied many times to RMB53 billion.

Based on "The Report on the Development Trend of Chinese E-Books in 2007," there were 660,000 e-books published and more than 300,000 were in widespread circulation. The number of readers on the market was 59 million and total sales income in 2007 reached RMB169, 400,000. Sales income of five publishing houses in 2007 hit RMB5 million, while 10 others sold more than RMB4 million.

Recently, with the rapid development of digital publishing has pushed traditional publishing to speed up its transformation. Until the end of 2008, 90% of presses had launched e-book publishing business and published 500,000 different e-books with income from them reaching RMB300 million. Some 300 newspaper had some kind of digital newspaper business with 9,000 kinds of digital periodicals and annual sales of RMB760 million.

The Commercialization of Publishing System Speeds up in an Improving Legal Environment

To satisfy the needs of economic development and international competition, changes have taken place in China's press and publication system and the reform has become fast and intensive in the past years. Presses are divided into two types, to either meet the public interest or for profit.

The later ones have gradually become companies and put in place modern operations that adhere to the law. "The Enforcement Program on the Deepening Reform of Publishing and Distribution System" stipulated by the General Administration of Press and Publications in 2006, encouraged publishing and distribution groups to hold stock of each other and take part in mergers and acquisitions. It also encouraged non-public capital to enter into industries approved by various policies.

In October 2006, Shanghai Xinhua Media Co. Ltd. went public through a back door listing, becoming the first press company in China to go public. After that, Sichuan Xinhua Winshare Chainstore Co. Ltd. listed on the Stock Exchange of Hong Kong. On December 21st, 2007, the Liaoning Publishing and Media

Established in 1937, the Xinhua Book Store has become a well-known culture brand with the largest book sale network in China.

Co. Ltd. went public in the Shanghai Securities Exchange, becoming the first state-owned cultural enterprise with editing and publishing business to go entirely public and become the top stock in China's publishing and media industry.

As of 2007, 23 publishing groups began to enter the capital markets actively through mergers and acquisitions. Reforms had been carried out in more than 100 bookstores and Xinhua Book Stores had undergone commercialization in 29 provinces, autonomous regions and municipalities directly under the Central Government. Some of those stores implemented a shareholding system.

There were 29 national chain publication companies and chain operations were implemented in 23 provincial Xinhua bookstores. Five book logistic centers with floor area of more than 100,000 square meters were set up in China. The annual profit of 10 book logistics centers was in the millions of RMB. There

The Beijing Book Building, located in the crowded downtown of Xidan, Beijing, is one of the largest book retail markets in China.

were eight national private chain companies and the number of distribution companies reached 100,000. There were more than 40 Sino-foreign joint ventures, Sino-foreign cooperation or foreign-invested distribution companies focused on books and periodicals. A network of distribution companies has grown rapidly and nine publishing and media companies have gone public with market capitalization of RMB200 billion and net financing of RMB18 billion. All these developments indicate that publishing companies in China have undergone profound changes.

"The Guidelines on Further Promoting the Reform of the Press and Publication System" was issued by General Administration of Press and Publication in April 2009, which presented a more specific route map and schedule for the reform of the press and publication system. It was regulated in the guideline that except for those in public welfare, the publishing houses of all the local and institutes of higher learning, engaging in profit-making service with books, audio and video products and electronic publications, must complete the work of transforming into enterprises by the end of 2009, and those of the departments and commissions under the central leadership by the end of 2010.

With the fast marketization of publications, laws affecting press and publications have improved. In 1990, the "Copyright Law of the People's Republic of China" was promulgated, it took effect in 1991. In the same year, the "Regulations for the Protection of Computer Software" were approved by the State Council. In 1992, China signed the Berne Convention and the Universal Copyright Convention, which marked the improvement of the publication law system of modern China and the integration with copyright efforts around the world. After that, promulgation of laws for the Chinese publishing industry was sped up. In 2001, to promote and meet the rapid development needs of the publishing industry, the Standing Committee of the National

People's Congress passed the "Copyright Law of the People's Republic of China."

Also in 2001, the State Council approved and promulgated the "Regulation on Publication Administration," the "Regulation on the Administration of Audio-Visual Products" and the "Regulation on the Administration on the Printing Industry." In 2008, the "Regulations for Administration of Publishing Electronic Publication," "Regulations for Administration of Making AV Products," the "Regulations for Administration of Books Publication" and the "Regulations on the Administration of Occupational Qualification of Publication Technologists" formulated by the General Administration of Press and Publication took effect.

On April 21st, 2009, the "Regulation on Legislative Procedure of General Administration of Press and Publication" was approved at the first meeting of the General Administration of Press and Publication. It was to take effect from June 1st, 2009. Until now, a system of publications with laws as the core, and based on administrative regulations as an effective supplement, has been created in China, shaping a law enforcement system protected by the judicial and administrative system that has played an active role in the protection of the sound development of Chinese publishing.

Publication Talent Groups have Enlarged with Remarkable Accomplishments in Professional Education and Research

High quality talent is the foundation for the rapid development of the publishing industry in which changes have taken place in terms of employees' structure and quality. A group of comprehensive talents have stood out. From 1978 to 1997, the annual rate of increase of employees in the industry was 11%. From 1998 to 2008, the rate reached 16%.

Meanwhile, publication education and research has grown fast, providing theoretical guidance and talent support to the prosperity of publishing industry. In terms of education for publications, from the 1980s, a complete professional education system of publications for multiple disciplines, levels and channels has been formed. Until 2008, undergraduate editorial and publication programs have been available in more than 70 universities or colleges. More than 40 universities or colleges offer postgraduate programs and 10 offer doctorate level programs. In terms of publication research, from 1977 to 1980, a new upsurge in the establishment of research institutions has been evident in different provinces, cities, autonomous regions, and 14 printing technology institutions have emerged.

In 1985, approved by State Council, the China Institution of Publishing and Distribution was set up (which changed its name into the Chinese Institution of Publishing Science in 1989). After that, different types of publishing research organizations have been established one by one and a network of publishing, printing, periodicals, newspaper, media and copyright research was gradually formed.

Many academic exchanges such as the International Publishing Symposium, the Annual Meeting of Chinese Edition Science and so on are held frequently. Every year, many academic achievements are made. Until 2008, 425 monograph textbooks and 38 types of periodicals were published. In addition, some professional academic networks comprising the Network of Chinese Press and Publication, the Network of Chinese Publishing and the Publication and Academic Network have become new platforms of academic exchange.

Publishing Industries in Mainland of China, Taiwan, Hong Kong and Macao have Bloomed, Forming the Pattern of Diversity in Unity for Chinese-language Publishing

While the publishing industry in the mainland developed rapidly, those of Taiwan, Hong Kong and Macao have also undergone great development. The pattern of diversity in unity of Chinese-language publishing has been based on the joint development of publishing in the mainland, Taiwan, Hong Kong and Macao.

The publishing industry of the mainland, Taiwan, Hong Kong and Macao play an active role in the spread of Chinese civilization as well as in the patterns of publication in the world.

At the Chinese-language publishing forum in the Frankfurt Book Fair in 2009, Vice-Director of the General Administration of Press and Publications Wu Shulin pointed out in his key-note speech named "Jointly Create a Bright Future for Chinese-language Publishing by Enhancing Tradition and Exerting Advantages," that Chinese-language publishing boasts a great cultural tradition, namely, the publishing philosophies of researching and applying what is experienced, drawing lessons from the ancient and perceiving reality, the publishing spirit of writing the truth and being loyal to history, publishing content that records history in a flourishing age with extensive knowledge and profound scholarship, the publishing of self-cultivation, of self-sacrifice and seeking perfection, the publishing organization supported and supplemented by the government and average people, the continual renovation and updated

The Macao exhibition in the Frankfurt Book Fair in 2009

innovation of printing technology, open-minded exchanges and various suggestions and opinions.

Chinese-language publishing has enjoyed a sound development based on rich resources from the long-standing and well-established Chinese civilization, the solid foundation offered by the elevation of comprehensive national power of China, the reliable power formed by the current scale and experience of Chinese-language publishing in mainland of China, Taiwan and Hong Kong, the huge market demand at home and abroad.

The Taiwan exhibition at the Frankfurt Book Fair in 2009

In the near future, Chinese-language publishing in mainland China, Taiwan, Hong Kong and Macao will experience greater development and play an increasingly significant part in the global publishing industry.

Road of Books

The Interaction between Chinese Publishing and the Outside World

The growth and development of Chinese civilization cannot be separated from its extensive exchanges with multiple civilizations. Ancient Chinese were passionate and active about learning all they could on the best foreign civilizations had to offer. At the same time, Chinese civilization spread to every corner of the world and promoted the spread of the Confucian culture circle. In these bilateral exchanges, the spread of publishing became significant.

In the long process of exchange, the well-known Silk Road emerged, as did the Road of Books. Through this road, China shared with the rest of the world papermaking and printing techniques while disseminating ancient science, technology and culture, which was a tremendous contribution to the development of human civilization. In the same fashion, foreign science and technology was also introduced to China, which in turn, had a huge impact on Chinese society and culture. The interaction between China and the outside world facilitated the development of Chinese publishing over the centuries.

The Spread of Papermaking Technique

Paper was already popular in China, at a time when many other countries and peoples continued to use ancient and primitive writing materials. For examples, Indians used palm leaves to transcribe scripture, Egyptians and Europeans used paper grass, sheepskin and wax paper.

As a medium for language, paper has unparalleled advantages. After the invention of paper making in China, it not only spread domestically but also found its way to foreign countries and, in a very short time, replaced local media and promoted the development of local publishing and cultural undertakings.

Initially what was exported was paper and paper products such as books, letters and paintings. Later, it was the paper

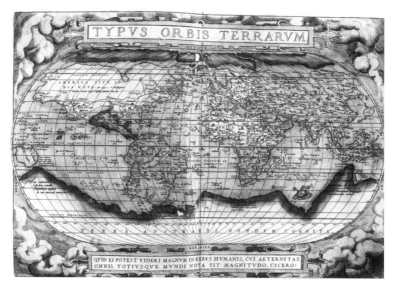

Theatrvm Orbis Terrarvm, compiled and prepared by Belgium cartographer Ortelius Abraham, was published in Belgium in 1570 and is the earliest European world map introduced to China.

making technology itself. The first recipients of paper and the technique were China's neighbors such as Korea, Japan and other countries in Southeast and South Asia. In the second century, Chinese manuscripts were exported to Korea and in about the third century, papermaking technique was introduced there and in Vietnam. From Korea, Chinese books were exported to Japan. In 610, Korean monk Tanzheng introduced paper making to Japan. In the seventh and eighth century, it was introduced to India. For example, during Tang monk Yi Jing's stay in India (671–694), the word "paper" already existed in Sanskrit. These countries, upon assimilation of this skill, gradually exported their paper products to China, which promoted economic and cultural exchanges.

Paper and papermaking spread to the Western world through sea and land. Around the second century, paper was brought to western cities like Heicheng, Dunhuang, Tunufan and Loulan. In the fifth century, paper was used across the central Asia region. In the eighth century, papermaking was introduced to the west. In 751, in a war between the Tang and Dashi (the Abbasid empire) in Talas (near Taraz in today's Kazakhstan), the army led by Tang general Gao Xianzhi (?–756) was defeated and thousands of Chinese soldiers were captured. Some of them were paper makers who introduced this technique to the Arabs in Samarkand (now Uzbekistan), which had rich cannabis and flax resources. A papermaking mill was established. Soon paper became an important Arab export to the west. This story was recorded in Arabian historical books. For example, the famous Arabian scholar Thaalibi (961–1038) once said that "of the specialties produced in Samarkand, what is worth mentioning is paper. It is neat, cheap, and suitable, so it replaced Egyptian paper grass and sheep skin. And such paper only existed here and in China." The author of the book *Journey and Kingdom* says paper was introduced by captive Chinese. These prisoners were owned by Ziyad, the son of Salibi. Some of them knew how to make paper. The production of paper not only met local demand and became an important commodity in trade. It met demand from around the world and is "a blessing to the whole world."

Later, between the eighth and twelfth century, Arabs established paper mills in Baghdad,

The scene in the European parchment workshop in the middle ages

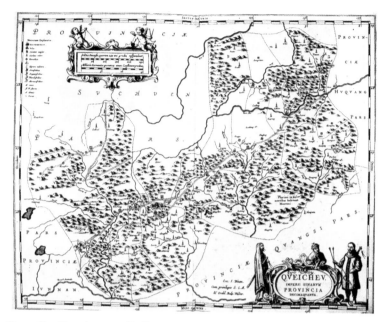

Novus Atlas Sinensi, prepared by European missionary Martin Martini, published in the Netherlands in 1655, the earliest maps of China published in the west.

Damascus, Egypt and Morocco. In 1150, Arabs reached Spain and established the first European paper mill in Xativa, in the north of Spain. By then, papermaking technology improved by Cai Lun had existed for over 1,000 years. In those times, the only people who mastered papermaking in Spain were Arabs and they monopolized the technique for 400 years from the eighth to the twelfth century. It was not until 1189, when the French established their own papermaking mill, that mills emerged in Christian countries.

Between the thirteenth and sixteenth century, many countries including Italy, Germany, the Netherlands, England, Russia and other countries built paper mills. In 1575, the first American paper mill was built in Mexico. In 1690, the first North American paper mill appeared in Philadelphia. It was not until the

Yongle Beicang, printed by the inner court in 1440, with concertina binding, standard script, and well printed edition.

nineteenth century that Melbourne, Australia, had its first paper mill. In about 1000 years, Chinese paper had spread around the world.

Once papermaking was introduced to Europe, local people attempted to improve the technique. Even in the seventeenth century, their skill was equivalent to that of the Song Dynasty. To address the problem of bad paper, the French minister of treasury A.R.J. Turgot (1727–1781) wanted to use Jesuits stationed in Beijing as spies to learn from the Chinese. In Emperor Qianglong's reign, the French missionary Benoist Michael (1715–1774), who was working in the imperial court, secretly copied the Chinese paper making technique and sent the details back to Paris, which led to the spread of advances in Chinese papermaking. In 1797, Frenchman Nicolas Luis Robert successfully invented machine papermaking. This was the first time Western papermaking technology overtook China's technology.

The Spread of Printing in Other Countries

China was the home of printing. When this great invention emerged, it soon spread to neighboring countries and later to west Asia, North Africa and Europe. Printing technology in most countries came from China, directly or indirectly. Some was built on the inspiration of Chinese printing.

Printing spread in Asia first. It was first popular to print Buddhist sutras and Tripitaka in particular. Korea, Japan, Vietnam and some other countries with long friendships with China and influenced by Chinese culture, used Chinese characters widely and believed in Buddhism. As a result, the printed Tripitaka became the most precious gift to these countries. Later, what was printed in China was not enough to meet their needs, so they learnt to print themselves, which helped spread printing techniques. Still under Chinese influence, printed books in these countries bear distinctive Chinese style. This did not change until the rise of modern printing.

Korea

Korea was among the first recipients of Chinese printing. In the seventh century, Korea often sent students to China, who returned with many books. Books were also exported to Korea as gifts or commodities, mostly Buddhist sutras. Chinese printing was also introduced to the Korean Peninsula thanks to the spread of Buddhism. It is difficult to determine the actual year this happened due to an absence of historical records. A reliable guess is the eleventh century.

In 993, at the request of the Korean kingdom, the North Song Kingdom gave the Buddhist Canon of the Kaibao Era as a

Ancient copper printing type of Korea exhibited in Gutenberg Museum of Germany

gift to this country. It was also probably during this time that Chinese type carving also went to the Korean Peninsula. Later, some people were sent by Korea to China to learn woodblock printing. They later became the first printers in Korea. Between 1011 and 1082, Korea reproduced Tripitaka for the first time.

After Bi Sheng's invention of the moveable type block printing, Koreans learnt this technique through the record of the *Dream Pool Essays* (*Mengxi bitan*). They built on this when they tried other innovative approaches such as using soil type, wood type, copper type, lead type and iron moveable type to print books. The most successful invention was copper type, which contributed to the spread and application of printing technology.

Japan

There is a very long history of exchanges between Japan and China. In 645, the Taika Reform in Japan started a wave of learning from China. Many envoys, monks and students were sent to China to learn Confucius culture and advanced technology. They returned with many articles, including copies

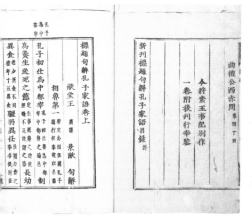

The School Sayings of Confucius printed with moveable type in Japan with similar style of Chinese books

Wood types from Japanese Enkoji Temple

of printed editions.

Woodblock printing was introduced to Japan during this process. It is said that around 770 copies, some 1 million volumes of the *Mantras of the Dharani Sutra* were printed and preserved in ten temples, where they are still kept today. Since these books do not have the date of printing, some Japanese scholars believe the printing was possible because of Chinese printing technology. The earliest block printed book with a recorded date in Japan was the *Doctrine of Mere Consciousness* in 1088, which was based on books from the Song Dynasty. Wooden and copper types were also used in Japan. Of the books printed in Japan, a large proportion were of Chinese origin and their content was similar to the Chinese originals.

Vietnam and Southeast Asia

As early as the Song dynasty, Chinese books were introduced to Vietnam in the form of gifts, such as printed Tripitaka and Daozang. Early printed books in Vietnam often dealt with Buddhism. The earliest recorded printed articles were household residency records printed between 1251 and 1268.

Chongning Wanshou Tripitaka, printed between 1080 and 1103, the first private printing of Tripitaka in China and the world.

In 1295, Vietnam received a Chinese-printed Tripitaka and later reproduced this book.

In the 1430's, the Vietnamese government started to print Confucian classics. In the seventeenth century, Chinese color registration was introduced. Print shops specialized in New Year painting also emerged in Hanoi and other places of Vietnam, both the theme, content and techniques employed in these prints all came from China. In the early eighteenth century, wooden moveable blocks were used to print books in Vietnam.

In the 14th century, many Chinese in the southeast coastal areas went to do business or settle down in the south pacific region. They brought with them paper, ink and books. Some Chinese craftsmen started printing businesses in Southeast Asia, which roused local interest in printing technology and promoted the development of printing.

Iran

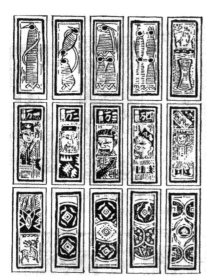

Printed paper card from ancient China

Paper money, paper cards and religious printed articles were introduced to west Asia during the Song and Yuan periods. They had the greatest impact on Iran. In China, Iran was called Anxi. Along with Persia, it had economic and cultural exchanges with China via the Silk Road. Persians were familiar with Chinese printing. They printed and issued paper money, modeled on the Chinese practice, in 1294. The money had Chinese and Arabian characters on it. In his 1310 Great Universal History, Persian historian Rashideddin gave a detailed description of Chinese woodblock printing, proving that Persians learned about printing from China. As a meeting place between east and west, Persia had many European merchants who also came to appreciate the significance, function and craft of printing.

Europe

With the westward movement of the Mongol armies, the link between China and west Asia, Central Asia and even Europe improved greatly and exchanges became more frequent. To kill time and to use as gifts back in Europe, many merchants often bought Chinese paper cards. Throughout the Crusades, many new things were introduced to Europe from the east, including paper cards, print painting and images. Many historians have noted that the soldiers fighting in the Crusades brought oriental block printing articles back to Europe.

Printed cards, paper money and religious paintings thus became the predecessors of printing technology in west

The existing oldest wood print in Europe: St. Christopher and Jesus from Germany.

Asia. French sinologist Abel Remusat commented that the shape, format and size of early paper cards in Europe were identical to what was used in China. Most were hand painted. Though paper cards are small, they use various techniques such as hand painting and wood block printing. They served as the most direct means for Europeans to learn the relevant technologies. What is more interesting is that because so many foreign paper cards were taken to Italy, the Venice government had to issue a directive prohibiting the import of printed articles from outside Venice in 1441. It has become a scholarly consensus that Chinese woodblock printing was introduced to

Early wood print Book of Revelation in Europe from about 1425

Europe between the late fourteenth and early fifteenth century.

After the Europeans discovered woodblock printing, they soon found type carving to be very cumbersome and not suitable to alphabet language. Therefore, block printing became more common. By the late fourteenth century, wood and block printed paper cards appeared in Europe. The earliest known wooden religious print in Europe was the *St. Christopher and Jesus* in 1423. In this German painting, St. Christopher is carrying a young Jesus across a river holding a cross in his hand. The left corner has mill wheels from China and two lines under the carving to the effect that whenever you see this image you will be spared the fate of death.

Block printed books first appeared in Europe in the 1440s. In terms of printing method, either words or images were carved in *intaglio* on a wooden block. A piece of paper was gently brushed on top of the ink painted block. The similarity of technique and raw materials to Chinese counterparts proves that European block printing was influenced by the east.

To Europeans, moving from woodblock printing to movable type block printing was not very difficult. The later system was particularly suitable to the Latin alphabet. The Uighur ethic group in Xinjiang, China, which lived in the meeting place between Europe and Asia and in the link to Central Asia, had developed wooden Uygur Script moveable type suitable for alphabetic language as early as the twelfth century in the Turpan region. This system served as a reference to the transition of Chinese moveable type to alphabetic language.

In the fourteenth century, many tourists, merchants and missionaries from Europe brought back information about moveable type block printing from China, so wooden movable type blocks appeared in Europe first. Swedish scholar Theodor Buchmann (1500–1564) in 1584 describes how wooden blocks were made in Europe: "Initially people carved all the words on one single block, which was very time consuming and costly, so later people used wooden moveable blocks, and then spelt them together to make a block." Wooden moveable block was a major link to the transition to metal moveable block.

It was against this background that the German Johannes Gutenberg started an in-depth exploration. Inspired by wooden movable type, he developed moveable type suitable for the European alphabet in 1450 using alloy made of lead, tin and antimony, which resolved in the long-standing problem of European language printing. He also invented a wooden printing press using screws to assert the pressure on the plate, instead of purely manual operation, which greatly enhanced the quality and efficiency of printing. Gutenberg's invention of printing was a re-invention based on Chinese printing. His invention quickly spread to various parts of Europe and changed the reality in which only nobles and monks could read and receive higher education. It also allowed for the production of material conditions for scientific advances and emergence of the European Renaissance.

Karl Marx believed that printing, gunpowder and the compass were "a necessary precondition for the development of the bourgeoisie" and is of enormous and far-reaching significance to Europe and the world at large.

Exchanges between Domestic and Foreign Books

China was both importer and exporter of books. Before 1840, China exported more than it imported, and was in the leading position in global publishing for a very long time, particularly with countries and regions under the influence of Confucius. The situation was reversed from 1840 onwards. Chinese publishing also declined in terms of printing. Under the impact of the western world, Chinese publishing underwent a major transformation in the late nineteenth century and enjoyed another period of boom.

China is the most advanced and influential Asian country in terms of printing. Since the third century B.C, cultural and economic exchanges between China and Korea, Japan, Vietnam, India and other Central Asian countries have been ongoing, and so was the exchange in books. For a long time, with the wide spread of Chinese culture, books from China were also exported in large volume to neighboring countries. This point has been analyzed above. The following part will focus on the introduction of western books to China.

Among the foreign books that came to China, Buddhist classics took up the lion's share. They were also the most influential. In the first and second century, Indian Buddhism was introduced to China through the Silk Road, so were Buddhist sutras. Since then, massive translations of Buddhist scriptures began and the exchange in publishing between China and foreign countries also boomed. Gradually Buddhist sutras became a major category in Chinese books. Translations were continuous from the third to the tenth century. In 971, the first Tripitaka in Chinese was printed, which included 1,076 Buddhist classics and 5,048 volumes. This project was repeated in the following dynasties.

Chinese version of *Dharani Sutra* from the Tang Dynasty unearthed in 1975, it is one of the early Chinese printed materials.

Sutras in Mongolian language: Fanjiazhuang.

By 1738, with the completion of Emperor Qianlong's version of Tripitaka (1,662 sections, 7,168 volumes), a total of 17 Chinese versions of Tripitaka were printed in ancient China.

The introduction of Buddhism had a huge impact on Chinese printing. First, it promoted the development of translation. Second, it gave full play to the role of printing. Third, Sanskrit texts printed on narrow traverse paper sheets inspired Chinese to move from the scroll-page format to album leaf format. Last but not least, Buddhism spread to Korea and Japan through China. Under Chinese influence, the former also engaged in massive printing of Buddhist scriptures, which promoted the development and exchange of culture and printing.

Books were not introduced to China until much later. Massive translation of these books did not start until the late sixteenth century when a group of European Catholic Jesuit missionaries began translations of their classics to preach. Between 1582 and 1757, over 500 missionaries came to China, and more than 70 participated in translation of over 400 books. Most of these books were on religion and the others on natural science and humanities.

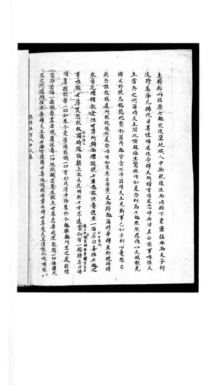

Christophori Clavii Bambergensis e societate Iesv, author Italian Father Matteo Ricci, moveable type printed Latin version in 1593, deposited in China National Library.

The publication of *Veritable Records of Catholic Saints* by Italian Father Michele Ruggleri in Guangzhou, in the year 1584 marked the beginning of foreign publication. From 1605, Chinese scholar Xu Guangqi (1562–1633), working with Italian Father Matteo Ricci and others, translated over 10 scientific works. Though what Matteo Ricci and other missionaries wanted from translation was to preach, their efforts actually brought useful knowledge to

Liber Organicus by Ferdinand Verbiest, inner court edition from 1674, the thirteenth year of
Kangxi's reign

China. For example, Original Geometry, a joint work by Ricci and
Xu Guangqi, is one of the earliest Chinese translations of western
natural science. *On Optical Tubes,* authored by J. A. Schall von
Bell (1592–1666) was the first western book on optics introduced
to China. *Illustrated Explanation of the Entire World,* written by
Ferdinand Verbiest (1623–1688) and *Atlas des Nations* by Matteo
Ricci opened the eyes of Chinese people to the world. *Outline of
the Human Body* and *Western Views of the Human Body* translated
by Johann Schreck (1576–1630) are among the earliest books on
physiological anatomy that were introduced from Europe to
China.

Book merchants in Qing Dynasty described by westerners

Bound by the Institute of Theology from the middle ages onwards, missionaries did not bring the most advanced ideas and science from Europe. However, they still introduced many fresh ideas to China. Unfortunately, in 1723 Emperor Yongzheng ordered all the western missionaries expelled from China, closing the door of western technical and scientific knowledge. For a long time, translation of these books came to a halt.

Intensive Exchange of Publishing between Home and Abroad in Modern Times

In the early years of 19th century, with the expansion of capitalism in China, western missionaries came to China again, bringing not only advanced printing machines to do publishing business, but also doing missionary works and introducing capitalism society through translating books. At that time, Chinese traditional publishing industry had declined and was left into the shade by western counterpart. Missionaries' arrivals mark the new times of translation of western books and exchange between Chinese publishing industry and that of the west which took on new look and features after the 1840s just as follows:

1) Translation works were published in large scale. Through books especially translation works, western thoughts and cultures came into China in large scale, exerting profound influence to the society and culture of China. New translation works were the main publications of church, government and private publishing agency, and translation works with large amount, wide content and great influence became the most important publications in Chinese publishing industry. According to the statistics, during more than two hundred years from 1528 to 1757, the type of books translated by missionaries in church were more than 400; from 1850 to 1899, the type of translation works published in China reached 537; from 1902 to 1904, the type of translation works were 533 equal to the amount of that in the half of 19th century.

In addition, based on Chinese scholar Xiong Yuezhi's statistics, from the first western book translated by Robert Morrison and

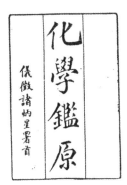 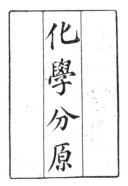 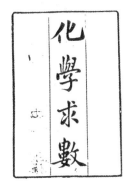

Translation works of chemistry published at the end of the 19th century in China

The portrait and photo of John Fryer, the Englishman with the most translation works who worked in Translation Department of the Jiangnan Arsenal for the longest time in China

published in China in 1811 to the end of governance of Qing Dynasty in 1911, 2,291 types of western books were translated and published in China during this period, which lead to the begin of the long-lasting movement of western learning spreading to the east. Centering on the subjects of "to know the world," "enrich and strengthen the country," "save the nation from doom and strive for its survival," "democratic revolution," "science and enlightenment," this movement exerted profound influence to the transformation of society in China.

2) Foreigners extensively participated in Chinese publishing industry. They opened book companies in China among whom were Robert Morrison, William Milne (1785–1822) and Ernest Major and so on, or they joined into the publishing agencies established by Chinese to do edition or publishing among whom were John Fryer, Young John Allen (1836–1907), Alexander Wylie (1815–1887) and so forth. They all made great contribution to the development and transformation of Chinese modern publishing

The written notes by John Fryer and the contract signed between him and the Jiangnan Arsenal

industry. According to rough statistics, nearly 60 printing agencies were set up by Christianity and more than 20 by Catholic Church. Meanwhile, lots of foreign employees worked in printing agencies set up by Chinese, such as the Beijing Translation School, the Translation Department of the Jiangnan Arsenal, Foreign Languages School and Commercial Press and so forth.

3) Part of publishing agencies began to adopt the operation model of Chinese-foreign joint. For example, Commercial Press invested jointly with Japanese companies from October 1903 with 100,000 Yuan invested by each part and 50% of the stock held by each part. Due to the jointly investment, Commercial Press became the first Chinese-foreign joint company in the history of Chinese publishing which played a significant role in the development of Commercial Press.

4) Chinese books and classics were introduced to abroad in large scale. These books were brought into Britain, France,

Germany, Russia, Japan, America, Sweden, and Holland and so on, and the main classics were translated into foreign languages and spread abroad. During the movement of "Western learning spreading to the east" taking part in China, the tread of "Eastern learning spreading to the west" was formed.

At that time, the breadth and depth of the exchange between Chinese and foreign cultures through books was unprecedented. In the process of modernization, Chinese publishing industry also presented unprecedented international features.

Copyright Trade and International Exchange in Publishing Industry in Contemporary Times

Since the founding of the new China in 1949, exchange between home and abroad in the publishing industry has become frequent, with a constantly strengthening opening-up policy and a steadily improving international level, the copyright trade developed rapidly for the past 60 years especially the 30 years of the adoption of reform and opening-up to the outside world policy. During this period, China has opened wider to the outside world and the international level increased stably. In 1992, China signed "Berne Convention" and "Universal Copyright Convention"; in 2003, matching the commitment which was made when China entered into the WTO, China opened printing industry and publication distribution service market. In 2006, distribution part of Chinese publishing industry opened in an all-round way to foreign capital. Until December 2007, distribution foreign enterprises approved by General Administration of Press and Publication were 62, 24 of which were solely-invested enterprise, 38 joint ventures.

Copyright trade is the product of the establishment and

improvement of socialism market economy after the adoption of the policy of reforms and opening-up to the outside world and the construction of socialism country governed by law. Since the 30 years of the adoption of the policy of reforms and opening-up to the outside world, the trade scale of Chinese copyright trade of books has changed from small to large, and publishing agencies and others major parts in the copyright trade has increased and become strong, which meant the transformation from bringing in books as the main part to introduce books to abroad actively in the trade. Besides, with the deepening of reforms and opening-up to the outside world, laws and regulations of copyright has improved gradually, and the environment of copyright trade and the policies of copyright trade will be conductive to the development of the industry.

Founded in 1986, Beijing International Book Fair (BIBF) has been held for 15 times, becoming the fourth international publication activities in succession to Frankfurt Book Fair, Book Exposition of America and London International Book Fair. The picture shows the scene of Beijing International Book Fair in 2007.

In terms of the amount, during the past 10 years, Chinese copyright trade has increased gradually on the whole. According to the statistics, in 2007, 11,101types of copyright of publications were brought into China, 10,255 of which were books, 270 sound recordings, 106 video recordings, 130 electronic publications, 337 soft wares and 1 other copyright. 2,593 kinds of copyright of publications were exported to abroad, 2,571 of which were books, 19 sound recordings, 1 electronic publication. The amount of export trade of books and periodicals, audio-visual products, electronic publications have increased by 140%, 73% and 112% compared with those of 2001 before the entry into WTO. In 2007, the proportion between copyright import and export for the mainland of China was 3.99:1. Moreover, based on the statistics, 16,969 kinds of publication copyright were brought into China and 2,455 types of publication copyright were exported in 2008. 15,776 types of book copyright were brought in, while 2,440 were exported with the proportion between copyright import and export 6.47:1. Although in an unfavorable trade balance, it still underwent a greatly improved situation compared with that of the past. In 2008, the top ten areas and countries for book copyright import were: Chinese Taiwan, America, Britain, Japan, South Korea, Germany, France, Singapore, Canada and Russia. The top ten areas and countries for book copyright export were: Chinese Taiwan, South Korea, Singapore, America, Russia, Germany, France, Japan, Britain and Canada. The two lists indicated the width of copyright trade.

On the whole, since 1995, the proportion between book copyright import and export has fluctuated. Before 2004 (except 1998 and 2002), the trade deficits of book copyright trade were above 10:1 with the highest 15:1. Since 2004, the deficits of copyright declined year after year, and the one of 2007 was 3.99:1, the lowest in the history, which can be seen from the chart below:

The total amount of book copyright import and export projects in China from 2001 to 2008

Year	Book copyright import	Book copyright export	Trade deficit	Import/ export
2001	8,250	653	7,597	12.63:1
2002	10,235	1,317	8,918	7.77:1
2003	12,516	811	11,705	15.43:1
2004	10,040	1,314	8,726	7.64:1
2005	9,382	1,434	7,948	6.54:1
2006	10,950	2,050	8,900	5.34:1
2007	10,255	2,571	7,684	3.99:1
2008	15,776	2,440	13,336	6.47:1

At present, China has actively imported the advanced printing technology and copyright from abroad, and continuously intensified efforts to introduce Chinese books to abroad. Under the guidance of the policy of "help China go to the world and let the world know China better," Chinese government has began to adopt the strategy of "going global" for the past few years which included "China Book International" and "the "Project for Translation and Publication of Chinese Cultural Works" held by General Administration of Press and Publication and Information Office of the State Council. Through the way of providing translation subsidy, these two projects aim to encourage publishing agencies in different countries to translate and publish Chinese books and help people in various countries know China better through reading books in their familiar languages. Recently, more than 20 countries and over 50 publishing agencies have applies for these projects for translation

China section in the Frankfurt International Book Fair 2009

subsidy. Additionally, with a continuous rise in the sales of publication abroad, China International Publishing Group and China Intercontinental Press have achieved a lot in external publication.

For the past few years, Chinese publishing industry have participated in different book fairs to publicize, exhibit and promote Chinese books, which continuously expanded influence of Chinese publishing industry and culture. Activities held by guest of honor in international book fairs have become an important stage for Chinese publishing industry to launch copyright trade and publicize Chinese culture. After Chinese publishing delegation took part in the Salon du Livre de Paris as guest of honor in 2003, it also participated in the Moscow International Book Fair and Seoul International Book Fair as guest of honor respectively in 2007 and 2008. In 2009, as guest of honor of Frankfurt Book Fair which was known as the "Olympic of Publishing Industry," China demonstrated the 5000-year splendid culture of China to the world through the stage of publishing industry and told the fundamental changes of China in contemporary times. The activity held by China as the guest of honor was a culture exchange with foreign countries with the largest scale, the highest standard and the greatest influence held by Chinese publishing industry in overseas since 1949. 272 publishing agencies from the mainland of China and 26 from Taiwan, China and 15 from Hong Kong, China with more than 2,000 participators and 7,600 exhibitions took part in the book fair in which 2,417 copyrights were exported. In addition, according to the official statistics of Germany, more than 290,000 people were attracted by the book fair, which promoted Chinese publishing industry to go global.

Among various international book fairs, the annual Beijing International Book Fair founded in 1986 and held for 16 sessions successfully has also played an active role in the promotion of publishing trade and exchange between home and abroad. Guided by the policy of "introduce foreign great books to China and let Chinese books go global to promote the international exchange of technology and culture and enhance the mutual understanding and friendship for all countries, the book fair has been among the top four international book fairs with the greatest influence in the world, which is the great event for Chinese publishers to strengthen the communication and cooperation with publishers from other countries. Due to this, this book fair is praised by more and more publishers from abroad as "a mirror for international publishing industry" and "an important name card for Chinese publishing industry."

From the 3rd to 7th, September 2009, the 16th Beijing International Book Fair with 43,000 square meters of exhibition area and 2,146 booths held successfully. 1,762 publishing agencies from home and abroad participated into the fair with more than 160,000 kinds of exhibited publications and rich exchange and culture activities as the main feature. Over 1,000 activities were held in or out of the exhibition hall during the five days with more than 200,000 attended person-times. Spain, the guest of honor with 1,000 square meters of exhibition area became high lights of this book fair. Nearly 70 cultural exchange activities with the exhibition subject of "Dream of Spain, think of Spain, interpret Spain" between China and Spain were held in which 30 Spanish publishing agencies, 15 writers, Chinese publishers and lots of readers participated. It was said that 12,656 intentions and contrasts of trade copyright were signed, 11,264 of which were copyright intensions, 1,392 copyright contrasts with the increase rate of 10.52% compared with that of last year.

In the future, Chinese government will keep intensifying and expanding policy support for expanding exchanges with other countries; and encourage publishing enterprises from home and abroad to expand the scope and the field of cooperation, enrich forms of cooperation and encourage them to create more great cultural products. At the same time, Chinese government will further intensify the campaign against copyright piracy and set up a copyright service system featuring low cost and quick trade to create a sound environment for the cooperation of publishing industry between home and abroad. It can be predicted that with the enhancement of comprehensive power of China and increasing contribution made by China to the world, the international level of Chinese publishing industry will be elevated and play an important role in the international publishing industry of the contemporary era.

Appendix I: A Brief Chronicle of China's Publishing Events

26th century B.C.: Appearance of Chinese characters.

21st–16th century B.C.: Appearance of primitive books and records.

1600–1046 B.C.: Beginning of primitive editing.

1046–771 B.C.: Government sets up specific book collections. Books and records appear.

770–256 B.C.: Private writing emerges. Confucius compiles ancient books and records.

213–212 B.C.: "Burning books and burying scholars alive"(*fenshu kengru*) by Emperor Qinshihuang.

2nd century B.C.: Invention of plant fiber paper and application for writing and painting. Early bookstores appear.

101 B.C.: Simaqian completed the first biographic style book *The Records of the Grand Historian*.

26–5 B.C.: The first large-scale state-level collection of books and preparation of state collection directory.

1st century: Introduction of Buddhism and Buddhist sutras to China. Buddhist scriptures translated.

105 AD: Papermaking improved by Cai Lun. Technique spreads across China.

175–183 AD: Carving of *Stone Classics of the Xiping Reign*, a large publication before the invention of printing.

7th century: Invention of woodblock printing, beginning of sutras and calendars using this technique. Bookshop and private printing emerges.

932–953: First government printing of the nine Confucian classics and first government-carved books.

971–983: First government printing of the Chinese version of the Chinese Tripitaka.

10th century: Invention of color woodcut printing.

1041–1048: Bi Sheng invents movable-type printing.

1048: The *Yongle Dadian Encyclopedia* is completed.

1561: Fan Qin encourages completion of *Tianyige*, the earliest known private book storage facility in China.

End of 16th century: Western missionaries involved in translation and writing in China.

1726: Compilation of *Gujin Tushu Jicheng* or *Complete Collection of Illustrations and Writings from the Earliest to Current Time.*

1782: Completion of *Siku Quanshu* (Complete Library in Four Branches of Literature).

Early 19th century: Involvement of foreign missionaries in Chinese publishing.

1840: Opium War starts. Western modern printing begins to penetrate China, leading to reform and transformation of Chinese publishing.

1897: Founding of the Commercial Press, marking the emergence of modern private publishing.

1912: Founding of the Zhonghua Book Company, ushering modern publishing undertakings.

1949: The 1st of October marked the founding of the People's Republic of China and the entrance into a new growth period for Chinese publishing industry.

1978: The compilation of "Encyclopedia of China" was launched. Until 1993, the first version of "Encyclopedia of China" was published.

1981: The first computer of China, Chinese character laser editing and composing system Huaguang I went through appraisal at the ministry-level, marking the Chinese publishing industry's entrance into the new age of "light and electricity" and the end of the age of "lead and fire."

1986: The first Beijing International Book Fair was held in Beijing. Until 2009, 16 sessions of the Fair have been successfully held.

1992: China signed the Berne Convention and the Universal Copyright Convention, which marked the improvement of the publication law system of modern China and the integration with copyright efforts around the world.

2009: As the guest of honor, China participated in Frankfurt International Book Fair in Germany, which effectively promoted Chinese publishing industry to go global.

Appendix II:
Chronological Table of the Chinese Dynasties

The Paleolithic Period	Approx. 1,700,000–10,000 years ago
The Neolithic Age	Approx. 10,000–4,000 years ago
Xia Dynasty	2070–1600 B.C.
Shang Dynasty	1600–1046 B.C.
Western Zhou Dynasty	1046–771 B.C.
Spring and Autumn Period	770–476 B.C.
Warring States Period	475–221 B.C.
Qin Dynasty	221–206 B.C.
Western Han Dynasty	206 B.C.–AD 25
Eastern Han Dynasty	25–220
Three Kingdoms	220–280
Western Jin Dynasty	265–317
Eastern Jin Dynasty	317–420
Northern and Southern Dynasties	420–589
Sui Dynasty	581–618
Tang Dynasty	618–907
Five Dynasties	907–960
Northern Song Dynasty	960–1127
Southern Song Dynasty	1127–1279
Yuan Dynasty	1206–1368
Ming Dynasty	1368–1644
Qing Dynasty	1616–1911
Republic of China	1912–1949
People's Republic of China	Founded in 1949